Dear Maureen,
Trust the light in your heart
to light the path before you.
Shine! Love,
Beth Wright

I and Eye

D1360322

A Guide to Vibrational Healing

and

My Transformational Journey to the Light

By Elizabeth Wright ©

"I and Eye" refers to the union of individual consciousness

with the Universal, Divine consciousness,

where we are all ONE.

Divine Phoenix Publishing

0

Copyright © 2012, by Elizabeth Wright
Published by Divine Phoenix Publishing, Skaneateles, New York

Cover Design by Cynthia Prado http://cynthia-prado.artistwebsites.com/
Cover Photo by Alexsandar Mijatovic

ISBN-13: 978-0985391522

A Note to Readers

I encourage you to contact me if you found this book helpful to you in any way. I would love to hear specifically how the book helped you in your own life or the lives of others so I can gather information for my next book. You can contact me at bwright66@hotmail.com

I am available to visit your town or city to teach Vibrational Healing workshops, all you have to do is ask.

Please visit my website at www.spiritworks.me

TABLE OF CONTENTS

ACKNOWLEDGEMENTS

A heartfelt thank you to my dear friend and soul sister, Laura Ponticello for all you have done for me. Thank you for your unshakeable belief in me and the book; for your faith that the messages within can help guide others to the light.

A deep thanks to my teacher, Fiona Clowes who taught me how to channel energy and connect with my Higher Self and to Rhonnda Elizabeth Stewart, for creating the Higher Self Connection Course that changed my life.

I also offer gratitude to my family and friends for supporting me and loving me exactly as I am.

I thank my Higher Self, Thomas for guidance, love and support and God for this beautiful gift of life.

DEDICATION

 While I was writing this book, two beautiful souls in my life passed away, my beloved father, Bill C. Wright and my faithful dog, Simba. My father died on October 16, 2008 and I was honored to be by him when his soul journeyed to the other side. He was 78 years old.

He died three years to the month after my mother. He was a wonderful father and raised me the best he could and for that, I will be forever grateful. He was a great man, a scientist, who earned his PhD from Cornell University in Agronomy and was an integral part of the Green Revolution in India in the 1960's. He lived his life with integrity, humor and dedication, and was a great role model. He possessed his own unique strengths and weaknesses, as we all do and in spite of those weaknesses, he always provided for me and loved me and after all, there is nothing more a daughter can ask for. I wrote this book sitting at his desk, which is a great honor.

My beautiful golden retriever, Simba, died three months to the day after my father on January 16, 2009. He was three  days shy of his 12th birthday. He was the best dog that ever walked the planet and was an enlightened being in a dog's body, my faithful companion and friend through all my trials and joys. Simba and I explored hundreds of miles together along the Australian coastline and in the woods of New York. He is with me now as my angel dog, still guiding and protecting me and when I walk I sometimes see a blue light bouncing along next to me and I know it is my precious Simba. I dedicate this book to both of them; I know my father would want top billing. I am honored to have shared time with them on this planet and thank them for all their gifts and love, forever and always.

PREFACE
What I Believe

I believe that human beings are all connected as One and we come from Spirit, or Source. If we remember that we are all One and connected and come from a loving, supportive Universe then we would never have a need to worry or engage in self destructive behavior or hurt each other.

Whatever I do to myself is what I do to you and whatever I do to you is what I do to myself, it is all the same. Everything is energetically connected and our thoughts and actions have a huge impact on those around us.

We are immersed in Spirit within and around us at all times. Once we remember and live our lives in this truth the world opens up and becomes a benevolent and supportive place.

I believe we each have come here to help each other in our soul's journey to evolve and that we have lessons to learn which can either be painful or joyous. I believe that in order to make the evolutionary process easier we must keep our minds and our hearts open, to allow for growth and that we must learn to let go of old or outdated beliefs that no longer serve us and align ourselves with the Truth.

Letting go brings freedom. By letting go, one would no longer feel the need to attach oneself to a person or outcome to be happy. Trust that whatever comes about is happening for the highest good. Believe that you are loved and loving beyond measure and this belief creates a beautiful existence. In this day and age we need to make it a habit to consider others and go beyond our own self. Some of us just think about our own happiness, health and prosperity or just our immediate family. But let's begin to cultivate the mindset to think about the well-being of all and act for the Highest Good of All.

First we must have the awareness that we are all connected to each other energetically and that we are in fact, one. Planet earth and all of her inhabitants is one giant organism. We all live here and share the planet and we all desire to live in a beautiful world where everyone is healthy and happy. So as one organism, it is beneficial for all of us to work in harmony together and treat each other, ourselves, our planet and all of its inhabitants with the utmost love and respect.

In yoga camp they gave a great example which I'll share with you. Let's look at how a human body functions. Each cell is an individual cell with its own job to perform; for example the cells in the respiratory system and the cells in the muscular system have very different jobs to perform. Yet, in spite of their different duties, each cell has a common goal, which is to provide health and well-being to the body. Just think of all the millions of cells that are doing their job so well every day just so you can exist, it's truly an amazing thought that most of us take for granted. The human body is an organism comprised of millions of cells that are working for its highest good every single moment. What happens if one of those cells decides it doesn't want to stay in order and work for the highest good anymore? Then we have a good cell gone bad and that's when cancer or disease begins in the body. That single "bad" cell begins to recruit other cells and the cancer spreads and there is no longer harmony and health in the organism, now there is disease.

Our world is pretty diseased at the moment, it's out of balance and there are many people, animals, environments and entire countries suffering from this imbalance. A lot of us feel that it is too far gone, too hard to change, impossible to start over and we feel powerless and hopeless with the injustices and imbalances that we see every day. However, there is something we can do. All is not lost. It begins with loving yourself first and then loving others and then spreading that love out to everyone we see and all the people we don't see, to all beings everywhere. Prayer and thoughts are extremely powerful energetic tools we can use to help heal the planet. Try this exercise:

1. Find a quiet place to sit uninterrupted for 10 minutes.
2. Connect to your Higher Self, just say hello and ask your Higher Self to connect with you.
3. Focus on your heart center and see a beautiful pink energy in your heart.
4. With intention send that pink love light out for the health and happiness of all beings everywhere.
5. Sit and feel the love light coming down from the Universe through your heart and out to all beings in creation. This will not deplete you, the love light is unlimited.
6. When you are finished, thank your God in whatever form that takes.

This is a very simple exercise that will expand the love in your own heart and will help raise the vibration of the entire population.

We can no longer deny that everything we do, every thought, every word and every action affects not only our self but others. Let us make a conscious effort to try our very best to be kind and loving in our thoughts, words and deeds. The future of this planet depends on it. I want to live in a beautiful world, I know we can do better than this, I know a brighter, golden age awaits us if we make it so.

PROLOGUE

Why I wrote this book:

I wrote this book to share the very important message that the Vibrational or Source energy of LOVE and wholeness is available to everyone. Knowing that this source energy of love is available to us is the most important piece of information I wish you to walk away with after reading this book. Believe in the existence of this source energy and then learn to tap into it. Once you open up to the energy, you are accessing a world of unlimited possibilities for change and transformation for yourself and the planet.

As you continue to invoke this love source energy, your vibration will continue to rise along with your consciousness. Your belief systems will start to change, replacing old, outdated beliefs that are aligned with your ego and false illusions of what society has taught you with Higher truths aligned with your divine self and God. As you start to see the truth in life, old triggers will no longer affect you. Your life will become more peaceful and calmer. You will begin to manifest the life you have always dreamed of. I have seen it happen through my own eyes, so if it can happen for me, it can happen for you too.

You are the only one who can make the choice to change. There are tools available to lift yourself out of a negative, sedentary state. It's a lot work, but oh so rewarding!

With regards to my personal life story, it's important to note that I recognize that my own story pales in comparison to the difficulties and challenges millions of others have had to endure in their own lives. I was never raped or abused, I didn't have to flee my country or lose my entire family in war; I didn't battle cancer or cut off my own arm to survive. However, everything is relative, and as a sensitive child I reacted strongly to the events in my life and they affected me greatly. Reflecting back, I recognize how many bad choices I made and so much difficulty and heartache could easily have been avoided, if I had just made healthy, positive choices. My choices came from a place of fear, from the wounded part of me, rather than a place of love, from my Higher Self. Some might say that I lacked strength of character and to be quite honest I would agree. I am learning to not be judgmental of myself because I know that it is pointless and only acts to separate me from myself. I can't rewrite my life story, I can only accept and forgive myself and move forward making choices based on love.

Growth can be painful, but it doesn't have to be. When staying the same is more painful than changing, you will change. No matter what crimes you have committed against yourself and others, this can be washed away with self love and forgiveness. When you get to a place where you truly see your wrongdoings and recognize the harm you caused, God will forgive you so that you can move forward and behave in a different way.

I understand that each person's journey is highly personal. It's all in your belief system which is supported by your vibration. Raise your vibration with the light and meditation, change your beliefs to align with the truth and everything wonderful and beautiful that you can possibly dream of will become available to you.

I remember feeling completely hopeless, shamed, depressed and despondent. I felt I was in a hole so far down that I could never crawl out. Let me tell you this, there is no hole deep enough that this universal love cannot pull you out of. I am here

to say, if I can do it, so can you. Believe.

SECTION 1 - Her Story - My Transformational Journey to the Light

Chapter One - All Messed Up & Nowhere to Go

"Faith is the strength by which a shattered world shall emerge into the light."
~Helen Keller

It was the Divine light that saved me; it was the light that changed my life.

I woke up one fateful morning in my bedroom in Sydney, my head pounding from too many drinks the night before, with a dim recollection of how I had gotten home. I went to get up out of bed and a shooting pain tore down my back; I screamed. I waited till my breath came back and I went to move again and the pain ripped through my body, sharp as before. I tried to shift my body weight several different ways, but each movement left me in severe pain. I realized that I couldn't move.

Even the tiniest movement to the left or the right left me in total agony. My eyes searched my room and I saw that I had made it home with my belongings from the night before, what a relief. My clothes were in a heap next to my bed on the floor. I started to recall everything I could remember, going to the bar with Kylie, dressed in heels and a tight dress, another night out in the bars which ended up in another hangover.

I was stuck like Kafka's cockroach, on my back in bed and unable to move an inch. I lay there till my flat mate walked down the hallway and I cried out for him to help me. He came in, hungover himself and listened to my curious tale of woe. He brought me some water and my cell phone and went on his way. I lay there all day unable to move till he came back. He brought me dinner and tried to help me move, but every time he tried to lift me, the pain was intense. He left me there alone and was good about it, trying not to make me feel any worse than I already did.

The night passed and the next morning came. I was hoping that when I woke up everything would be back to normal, but still I could not move. Somewhere in the 30th hour of this saga, I began to search deep within. I couldn't drink a beer, smoke a cigarette, run on the beach or watch TV to escape. I was stuck there, just me, my sober mind and my conscience.

My mother had passed away suddenly & unexpectedly two months before. She had died overnight on October 29th, 2005 sending shockwaves throughout the family. I was swimming in grief and barely keeping my head above water. I was drowning my sadness in alcohol, my best friend and wondering what was the point of all of this?

I had been in Sydney eleven years and my mom had wanted me to come back to the United States. I had almost moved back that March, but decided to stay on to pursue my life, if that's what you wanted to call it. I was running away from my family, myself and shirking all responsibility. Now she was dead and I hadn't been by her side. I had only seen her a handful of times in the past eleven years. The guilt was all-consuming.

Tears flowed freely but I couldn't cry too hard otherwise the pain in my back would start to spasm. I took a good hard look at my life, lying in bed, at thirty nine years of age; I summed it up with this: I spent thirty nine years trying to live my life "my way" and made an absolute and utter mess of things. The few good friends I had surrounded myself with, like me, loved to party hard, I didn't have a romantic partner, or children, no career to speak of, no purpose I was passionate about, I owned no property and I had no family nearby to care for me. I was living a superficial life, jumping from job to job, man to man, with a rather large credit card debt and nothing to show for it. I was not the person my parents had raised me to be. I knew I was so much better than the life I was living. There was a giant hole inside my heart. Is this what I wanted for myself? Is this the life I was destined to lead? The answer was a big "No".

I was disgusted with myself, deeply ashamed, sad, sorry and afraid. With tears in my heart, I called out to God, The Universe and told him that I was going to turn my life over to him, that I had made a mess of things. Now I was surrendering my entire life to what he wanted me to do. I prayed for help in turning my life around.

In that moment, with conviction, the decision was made to return to United States, live with my sister in New York and change my life. It was never something I wanted to do, but now I knew it was the right thing to do. I knew that this was God's plan for me. I had been in this place before; wanting to quit partying for years and I had tried and gone two or three months, but this time it was different. I couldn't keep living this same lifestyle, my spirit was dying, my soul was crying out for change.

I had a failed marriage, failed jobs, failed relationships as people didn't respect me because I didn't respect myself and now my mother was dead. My life was a failure and I was unhappy and I didn't love myself. My skin was dry, my hair was thin and my eyes were shrunken and bloodshot. My kidneys ached most of the time and I had bladder issues and weird pains in my body. I knew that if I continued down this road I would end up dead, if not in body, in spirit. In that moment, I surrendered and changed my life forever.

Thirty minutes later two paramedics pulled me out of bed and got me to the hospital and the mere act of standing up and walking around seemed to shift my spine back into place.

When the nurse practitioner came to see me I was disheveled and tears were flowing down my face. I told her of my despondency over the loss of my mother, that I was lost and couldn't see the point of living anymore. They say that depression is not a character flaw, it is a chemical imbalance. She looked at me with true compassion, a slender, smart woman about my age and exclaimed, "Oh honey, I wish I could take you home with me." Like a stray cat that needs a warm home and a bowl of milk. She meant it too. I walked out of that hospital in the next half hour with no pain in my back at all, as if the entire incident had been fabricated from thin air.

Although I had surrendered my direction to God, I refused to do the hard work just yet. I decided to drink my way out of the country like I had lived most of my adult life, totally lacking in grace and self-respect. This behavior stemmed from a feeling within that I was not worthy, not valuable. Most of my life, I believed this lie and acted accordingly, with such a force of self destruction that I nearly poisoned myself to death.

Only by the grace of spirit within, my Higher Self, did I pull out of this death spiral, and for that I am forever grateful.

As a child, I was blessed to be born with an open heart and an open mind. I was born a free spirit. I knew the truth about us all being One, but my education within and out of school taught me that I was separate. Events in my life caused me to store pain and fear deep within my body. My fear-based life caused me to self-destruct and I learned to make choices and live my life based on the fear. It wasn't until my mid-30's that I reconnected with the Divine and began to turn my life around. Through an energetic healing course I took in Australia where I lived for eleven years, I reconnected with my Higher Self, the most perfect and spiritual part of me. Our Higher Self wants us to reach our highest potential and transform from ego-consciousness (me, mine, I) back to God consciousness (oneness) and will guide us to this place if we allow it. It took me several years of hard work to heal my past, to work through the shame, guilt and unforgiveness and learn to love, respect and trust myself. I now live my life in love with purpose and passion. My wish, hope and purpose is to help others remember and understand the truth of who we are.

We are meant to enjoy (in joy) our life on earth!

Chapter Two - The Challenges of an Indigo Child

"Keep me away from the wisdom which does not cry, the philosophy which does not laugh and the greatness which does not bow before children."

~Kahlil Gibran

I was born an "indigo child", which author and consultant for gifted children, Wendy H. Chapman writes about on her website www.metagifted.org : "The name itself indicates the Life Color they carry in their auras and is indicative of the Third Eye Chakra, which represents intuition and psychic ability. These are the children who are often rebellious to authority, nonconformist, extremely emotionally and sometimes physically sensitive or fragile, highly talented or academically gifted and often metaphysically gifted as well, usually intuitive, very often labeled ADD, either very empathic and compassionate or very cold and callous, and are wise beyond their years. Indigos have come into this world with difficult challenges to overcome.

Their extreme levels of sensitivity are hard to understand and appreciate by parents who don't share this trait. Their nonconformity to systems and to discipline will make it difficult to get through their childhood years and perhaps even their adult years. It is also what will help them accomplish big goals such as changing the educational system, for instance. Being an Indigo won't be easy for any of them, but it foretells a mission. The Indigo Children are the ones who have come to raise the vibration of our planet! These are the primary ones who will bring us the enlightenment to ascend."

I was always a very sensitive child and from a young age. I was a gymnast when I was young, gifted with great flexibility and this sport helped me develop great focus. I spent most of my childhood upside down on my hands. I was very good at most sports I tried, including diving, swimming, volleyball, tennis, softball, skiing and cheerleading. I placed 3rd in State on the local diving team in Westport, Connecticut after diving for two years. Both my mother and father had been natural athletes and they passed some of those genes onto me. I was also artistically inclined with a good eye and I loved to draw as well as sing. I was in the chorus and choir and played the French horn for a few years in band and orchestra.

I was book smart; I did well in school and was a popular student. Although numbers eluded me, I excelled in English and Science. I had a natural attractiveness that people appreciated with blonde hair, blue eyes, a pretty smile and an athletic body.

Even as a child, I was able to see into people, to see and feel their pain. I was also able to recognize their incongruity, when their words didn't match their actions. I noticed that some people would pretend to be "fine" when really they were hurting and unhappy inside. When I picked up this incongruity in an adult, the wise child inside knew that she didn't want to obey this person because they weren't standing in their truth, so it didn't make sense to me to follow their commands. This rebellious nature caused me grief with authority. I wanted to escape from this world of adults that were full of lies.

As a child, I didn't see the point of the rules and systems that our society had put in place. So many rules seemed to be in place just for the sake of having a rule, the intent was not pure, and it didn't make sense, it was simply "going by the book". The systems seemed to clump all people together like sheep, without allowing for true self-expression, creativity and growth to shine through. I could easily see what wasn't fair and these systems angered me. I was told by my mother, "Life is not fair" and it seemed that the sooner I accepted this fact, the easier my life would be, so that I would just follow along, like all the other sheep, in a state of learned helplessness. But it seemed quite obvious to me that a better way would be to change what is not working for the people. Why not change it if it doesn't make sense?

I was brought up in a time where I was expected to finish school, then University, get married, have children, work in a career, pay taxes, own a home and then retire with a hobby until the end of my life. This was the model that was presented to me by my parents and society. Something deep inside of me knew that this was all an illusion. I could see the pain behind those people who were supposedly successful, with big houses, great careers and 2.5 children. Half of the men my father worked with had left their wives for their secretaries. The wives were devastated and bitter and left to mourn for their marriages. I remember thinking that the "model" didn't seem to work for everyone; it was not a win-win situation. Therefore, I did not believe in the model, but did not have an alternative model to ascribe to. To me, the world I lived in was a sham; therefore, I decided not to play by the rules.

I strongly rebelled against authority, but my father's strict principles kept me in fear of expressing this rebellion outright. It was very much a household of tradition; obey your elders even if they aren't right, you just do it because you were told to do it.

Being an indigo was a challenge for me because I felt like an outcast, like I didn't belong because the people and systems weren't aligned with what I instinctively knew as the truth. I was brought up with the model of competition, which ends with a winner and a loser. Having winners and losers doesn't feel good; it creates a feeling of separation. Why can't we all be winners? To avoid feeling bad, I learned to win and I was rewarded for my accomplishments. This behavior pleased my parents and teachers so I replicated this behavior over and over, growing my ego and my separation from self. A fear of losing was installed in me and I felt squashed and disconnected from who I truly was as well as from others.

Strangely enough, as a young child, there was a feeling deep inside that told me that one day I would do something important. I didn't know how, but I just had an assuredness that my role in this lifetime was valuable for helping the population of this planet stand in their truth.

At the age of thirteen, an event took place which caused a separation from myself. It was this separation from self that was one of the causes of my internal pain and helped to create my self-destructive pattern. I started to dislike who I was, which was a mirror image of those around me. I started drinking at the age of fourteen. This was a great way to escape from myself, to get away from the person I didn't like, the person who held the pain. But as Bob Marley sings, "You can't run away from yourself."

Chapter Three - The Early Days - Family History

"One must have chaos in oneself to give birth to a dancing star."
~Nietzsche

Growing up, my family life was fairly chaotic. My parents moved to New Delhi, India in 1963, where my father had taken a position with the Rockefeller Foundation in Agricultural Research and Development. I was born in New Delhi on November 25, 1966. We had a big house and seven servants. My mom got to throw fabulous parties for all the other expat families and play golf, winning the Northern Women's golf championship in 1970. Her name is still on the plaque in the New Delhi golf club.

Meanwhile, my dad worked at a job teaching the farmers of this third world country how to yield more grain per acre using scientific knowledge he had gained from his PhD in Agronomy from Cornell University. My parents were young, talented and loving their life in a foreign land thousands of miles away from the unrest of the revolution taking place back in their homeland in the 1960's, which they had escaped. They were at the top of their game and they worked hard and played hard, enjoying life and grabbing life by the horns.

Before we were born, my mother had given birth to a boy who had holes in his heart, he was a blue baby. He died three months after birth and both my parents were devastated. I don't think my mother ever got over that event, I think it broke her heart.

When I was a baby in New Delhi, I used to hang out with the servants. If my mom couldn't find me she would go look in their quarters and there I would be with a mango seed in my mouth or a ring of chili around my mouth, saying, "I eat chili mommy." I was a tow-headed child and quite the attraction to the Indian people who always wanted to carry me. Consequently, I didn't learn to walk till I was two years old. My nickname was Goodja, which meant "little doll". I recall my last day in India at three years old, driving away from the house with a garland of marigolds around my neck and waving goodbye to the servants.

In 1970, my father took a position in Ankara, Turkey where we relocated for the next seven years. We had a great apartment and my parents hobnobbed with all the other bright and talented

Americans and British who were Fulbright and Rhodes scholars; diligently working to change the world for the better. They went to grand parties at the embassies, met diplomats and we travelled all over the world.

I had been around the world three times before I was ten years old. We had airplane stories galore that never ceased to amuse back in the days when flying airplanes was a glamorous affair. I was so lucky to have seen the world at a young age; it gave me a good perspective at the outset. We moved back to Hyderabad, India for three months when I was eight years old.

I remember one of our servants died and they burned his body in a funeral pyre, a pile of firewood, at the bottom of the driveway and no one made a big deal out of it. I also remember seeing our sweeper lady's brand new baby wrapped in a dirty cloth in the servant's quarters which was nothing more than a mud and straw hut on our property. My parents gave them the standard cup of rice for a birth gift. To see poverty at such a young age was a gift, for I was able to see firsthand that this is how most of the world lived their life, struggling daily to put food into their mouths. I also saw how joyful these people were even without material possessions.

I had a rebellious brother who caused a lot of unrest in our family. My brother is a gifted artist. His mind works differently allowing him to see things from a unique abstract perspective. He was also a great athlete and an attractive kid with charisma. However, his relationship with our father was difficult. My father totally embodied the left-brained scientist and was raised in a poor family from Mississippi. My brother took his anger over this rejection out on me and my sister in the form of verbal and physical abuse. He took away my peace at an early age and created chaos. My brother was also self-destructive and I learned that behavior from him.

My father either adored or ignored me because I was the youngest. He was an excellent provider and always made sure I had everything I needed in the material world. He was however, emotionally unavailable, which is quite common among fathers of his generation. It seemed to me that he felt he failed as a father because so many of his colleagues had children who were on their way to becoming doctors, engineers & scientists and his own children were not following the traditional path of success as he defined it. He did love us, however.

My sister didn't take any nonsense from my brother and tried to protect me from him, but I would go back to him again and again just for the attention. Caught in the middle was my poor Mom, trying to be the peacemaker with a stubborn husband who wouldn't give an inch and a frustrated son who acted out in any way he could just for attention. I was the baby and I used to cry just to keep my brother away from me at times. I learned how to turn on the tears for self-protection. Everyone in my family told me I was too sensitive and my nickname became cry-baby or Brathy - for brat because I was spoiled.

I experienced the biggest culture shock of my life when in 1977 at the impressionable age of ten, we moved from Turkey to Westport, Connecticut. Westport is probably one of the more affluent towns in the country now and was certainly on its way in 1977. I moved from a community which was comprised of a group of open-minded, intelligent, tight-knit Americans who all banded together in a foreign country and the delightful Turkish people to a wealthy, old-moneyed suburb on the East Coast of

America. Here everyone lived in huge houses behind closed doors in an isolated environment.

To me it was going from an earthy, worldly, soulful community to a status-driven, competitive world where money was power. It was a whole different world and a place where in the five short years we lived there, my family suffered greatly.

My father was working out of the New York City office and commuted two hours by train each day. My mother was left in the suburbs with the kids and no friends. Her talents were lost here and she had trouble connecting with other wives and mothers. She had an inferiority complex around money as she was raised in a poor Texan family and to be thrown in with these blue-blooded, well-groomed women was detrimental to her self-esteem. She didn't ever feel that she was "good enough" to begin with and in Connecticut, the feeling was exacerbated by social status. My father was taking three month trips to Africa on assignment leaving my mom to raise three teenagers by herself.

My parents both enjoyed alcohol and used it daily. One of my parent's favorite sayings was "the sun is over the yard arm somewhere in the world". They were part of the brat pack generation, a time when most people of their stature found it socially acceptable to drink regularly. I learned early on that alcohol was how you relaxed during the week and how you had fun in social settings. My brother started to dabble in drinking and drugs. My sister and I were glued to the television since we'd never had one before and we spent hours watching *Mary Tyler Moore, I Love Lucy, Mash, The Love Boat* and *Charlie's Angels* while stuffing our faces with Twinkies and other junk food we didn't have access to overseas.

It was around this time that I noticed my mother changing; she started to spend more and more time in bed and was drinking more. She was depressed and not coping well. She didn't understand depression and she blamed her feelings on her unsupportive relationship with her mother and my father. She had become a victim.

Shortly after my 13th birthday I remember coming home from school to find a totally empty house. There was a note on the kitchen counter that said something like, "Your mother is in the hospital. I will be home later, make yourself dinner. Love, Dad."

We found out that evening that mom had had a "nervous breakdown" and had tried to kill herself. The news left me numb, I didn't understand and I was confused. It was this very event that had a huge affect on every part of my being.

My mother was the center of my universe. She was my role model, the voice in my life and the principle love-giving human in my world who was guiding me and shaping me and caring for me. She had for most of my life been a successful leader and winner who others admired and aspired to be like.

Now she was lying in a psychiatric hospital with no desire to live. It didn't make sense and my own self worth and identity was greatly affected. If she didn't want to live, what was the point of me trying? Didn't she love me and want to be my mom anymore? I believe I dissociated at that time and a part of my psyche broke away. I was, up until then a confident, sensitive child, with a strong will and knew who I was and what I wanted. Now I felt lost, disconnected and confused.

My life lost meaning. Within that same week, I began my menstrual cycle for the first time and my sister had to explain the whole female process to me. For thirty years after I always had trouble with my cycle, I never knew when it was coming and I was always having "accidents". I was always sort of shocked when it arrived. I always had huge emotional hormonal freak outs before my period, which a therapist later told me I was recreating on a subconscious level, to mimic the original event, a time of chaos and disconnect.

Following my mother's hospitalization, my father found it difficult to communicate with us about what was happening. He was emotionally unequipped to discuss such matters with his teenage children. My sister decided my mother was weak and that she would never be like her. My brother blamed himself for being such a difficult child. I decided that I must not be valuable if my mom didn't want to be here anymore. She was in and out of the psychiatric hospital for two years and given strong medication, shock treatment and attended therapy and AA. She was not the same mother. The guiding light was gone and in its place was an insecure, sick and angry woman who blamed others for her sickness. Her light was replaced by darkness. She shared all of her misaligned thoughts and inadvertently passed her paranoia and insecurity onto me and I was taught that other people were out to get you. I couldn't talk to anyone at school about it because I was deeply embarrassed and ashamed.

I felt inferior. I turned fourteen shortly after and I went to a friend's party where there was alcohol. I drank straight vodka for the first time and caused a huge scene by running down the street and boys had to chase me and pin me to the ground to control me. I puked all over my friend's carpet and woke up feeling awful. The next Monday in school one of the boys told me that everyone was talking about me and that I had just acted that way to get attention. I denied this vehemently, although I think it was true, but now I realize that the attention I was seeking was for someone to help me with all that was going on in my life. After that, I began to drink at other parties and alcohol made me do wild things.

I loved the feeling of being out of control. My body reacted to alcohol and made me feel uninhibited, like I could do anything. This was a place with no limits, which was congruent with what I knew to be the truth, life was supposed to be limitless. The only problem was that this limitless existence was only available in an altered state. I didn't know how bad it was for me at the time. It was a great escape. I hated how I felt the next day but not enough to stop. Still, I did well in school and sports and was popular. I was totally infatuated with boys but scared of them at the same time, never forming real friendships with any of them.

Then in 1983, after my sophomore year of high school, my father was looking to transfer out of the states again to take an assignment in Indonesia. My sister left for college, my brother was already in college and my mom was on the mend. The Rockefeller Foundation didn't want to send my dad overseas with an unstable wife, consequently the assignment in Indonesia never materialized. Westport was eating up all of my father's hard earned money and he decided to take a sabbatical at North Carolina State University in Carey.

I moved there with my folks and started my junior year living in the South East which was so very different than the North East Coast. It was another culture shock and I had only one good friend and no siblings and my parents had given our dog to my Aunt. Once again, I was leaving everything and everyone I knew to start over at the vulnerable age of fifteen. I bonded closely with my parents and I remember enjoying that aspect of it. I got them all to myself and I got to see my dad more than I ever had in my life. Mom was becoming more like her old self again.

The next year we moved to Stillwater, Oklahoma where my dad took a job at Oklahoma State University as Assistant Dean of Agriculture. This was my fourth high school in four years in three different states. Again, I was the new kid on the block in unfamiliar territory.

Oklahoma is right smack in the middle of the Bible belt and everyone talked so darn slow, even though they were smart, it sounded like they were dumb to me. It was my senior year and I found a friend that was into partying. We used to go to a local bar and it was here that I found kindred spirits. All of the staff I hung out with at the bar were older than me but they were so much fun and relaxed and seemingly adventurous.

By the time I was legal I started working there and my partying blossomed. I also started to dabble in drugs, trying out MDMA, which was legal at the time and it only cost $3. I loved this drug!

I remember venturing out to a frat party all buzzed up by myself one night. I met a boy and was doing backbends over the second floor balcony, holding onto a piece of wood on the side of the building, needless to say, there was no railing. I fell off the balcony upside down and managed to flip around in the air and landed feet first onto soft ground. I had the wind knocked out of me and was scared to death. I was so drunk I didn't recognize how lucky I was that I didn't break my neck. A year earlier, in a horse accident, I had jumped off a horse that I wasn't in control of and landed on my left hip. These two injuries, a year apart, really damaged my spine which affected my entire central nervous system.

In 1984, after I graduated high school, I decided to go to the University of Colorado, Boulder for my college education. I loved English and I liked to write so I decided to study Journalism. Dad had finally secured another overseas position with IAD, the International Agency of Development in Islamabad, Pakistan and I went over there with them the summer before my freshman year. It was an exciting time but I do remember feeling scared that soon I was going to be all alone with no family.

Chapter Four - Growing Pains

"It is always the false that makes you suffer, the false desires and fears, the false values and ideas, the false relationships between people. Abandon the false and you are free of pain; truth makes you happy, truth liberates."

~Sri Nisargadatta Maharaj

My parents took me to Boulder and settled me in to my dormitory before returning to Pakistan, thousands of miles away and seemingly inaccessible. I was just seventeen years old but still stuck in the emotional body of that scared and confused thirteen year old. I found out an old friend from Westport was also going to be living in the same dorm as me.

My drinking really took off at Boulder and I also discovered drugs. It was here I met my first boyfriend, Max. He was an adventurous boy from San Francisco and we had lots of fun together. We had a group of friends and we used to all hang out and party as well as spend time in the glorious natural surrounds of Boulder.

I was introduced to cocaine and ecstasy. I loved both of these drugs because I could drink more and be somewhat coherent on them. There was also marijuana, which never agreed with me but I smoked it anyway because it was there and everyone else was doing it. Then there was mushrooms and acid, which were wonderful for expanding the mind. I had one particularly bad trip on acid and the next day someone wrote a message for me on my dormitory door that said, "reality is made for people who can't handle drugs."

It's important to note that I didn't just party in college, I studied and worked, danced, created art, played sports, hiked and skied in the beautiful mountains and enjoyed a lot of my life. It's not as if my whole life was about drinking and drugs and being depressed, it is so much more than that. I have done amazing things, traveled all over the world and met wonderful people. In all of my pictures in my albums you will see smiling, happy people enjoying their lives. For me, it was my inner life that suffered from the pain I carried from my childhood and I used drinking and drugs to numb the pain. Once I became addicted, I was physically and emotionally imbalanced after continued abuse of the substances I ingested.

Most young people party, it's a pretty normal phenomenon. As we reach our late twenties, thirties and forties, we learn that partying is something to be enjoyed on occasion and we slow down. For those that don't know when to stop or slow down, there are usually underlying issues that need to be healed, just like with me. I know there are millions of people out there who are similar to me.

It took me four years to complete my Journalism degree and I was graduated in May of 1998, at twenty one years of age. I graduated with a decent grade average and lots of friends but without any sense of what I wanted to do with my life. I had zero interest in becoming a journalist as I didn't really respect the media in America.

I recall looking on the board at the Journalism school where they posted which jobs were available and there was a production internship in Scottsdale, Arizona for a TV station which held no appeal to me whatsoever.

I felt very lost and when I looked out into the future all I saw was a foggy mist. Now what was I supposed to do? This didn't make any sense at all to me. In Boulder, there is a school called Naropa, which teaches the healing arts and I was always curious about it but I never once stepped foot in the building. Looking back I can see that Naropa was most probably my next step, but my fear kept me from going in that direction.

My folks were still in Pakistan and the rest of my family scattered about. My friends all had their own plans and were heading in different directions. Again, I felt abandoned and alone. The only lead I had was that my sister had lived in Martha's Vineyard for the previous summer and raved about it. I decided I would go live there for the summer while I figured out what to do next.

After college at Boulder, I spent nine months on Martha's Vineyard and then I moved to Vail, Colorado where I learned to be a great skier and also a partier. When I wasn't enjoying the absolute stunning beauty and natural wonder of the Rocky Mountains, I got a reputation as a lush. It was there I met my future husband, a very fun-loving and genuinely nice Australian man. I was attracted to him because he was well-liked, down-to-earth, fun and responsible. I desperately needed stability and grounding in my life and I thought he could provide that for me.

After a year of dating, his visa expired and he invited me to join him in Australia. I was terribly irresponsible and really wanted to just escape my life in Vail. Without meaningful work to focus on or any spiritual path, my sense of self came to me by the man I was with at the time. I quit my job as a waitress, sold my car and went there without telling my parents until after I had left. Needless to say, when they heard the news, they were not impressed.

I stayed with him in Oz for a few months and then returned to stay with my folks in Arkansas. After I was there for a month, my boyfriend called and asked me to marry him. I guess he realized he missed me and he also wanted to return to live in Vail, which was a fun and adventurous lifestyle. We were both young, I was only 24 and he was 22. We got married in Vail in 1993 and had a fun wedding, which both our families attended.

I actually pulled myself together pretty well at that time, I had real hope that this would be good for me, for us and that we would have a strong future together. If I had cleaned up then and focused on a purposeful life for myself, things may have worked out for us. However, I still lacked clear direction. I was still

48

missing that all important connection to myself. I still needed to fill the hole inside, but had no clue how to do it. The only way I knew how to feel better temporarily was to numb myself; this is called self-medicating.

After three years in Vail, we decided to leave for Australia and try our luck back in his home town. Once we got there, the excitement of the change kept me happy for a while. I still carried all my pain and had not healed, and consequently I recreated the same meaningless existence for myself, only this time I was thousands of miles from my family and quite depressed.

My husband didn't know what to do for me and became increasingly frustrated with my behavior; consequently, he spent more time away from me. I hadn't found a line of work that interested me and that was not something he could fix. I just couldn't see what it was that I wanted to do in the rat race, nothing interested me; life was all bullshit and more importantly, I didn't want to be a rat!
I continued to drink daily and I was crying and complaining a lot. After three years, I left for the States because I wanted to end the marriage, since I felt my husband couldn't make me happy. That

49

was one of the problems; I was expecting him to make me happy instead of trying to make myself happy.

I stayed in New Mexico with my brother for three months and after that, I decided to go back and give it one more try. After being back a few months I realized it wasn't going to work, we still didn't know how to communicate with each other and my emotional needs weren't being met. He spent most of his time away from me involved in sports clubs or with his mates and I felt unloved.

It was at that time that I met a devilish and charming man at work. I wasn't attracted to him at first but his charming, naughty ways made me laugh. He had heard through a friend at work that I was unhappy in my marriage and he invited me for a drink. I said no at the time but I remember making the decision to go meet him for drinks one afternoon while my husband was with his friends. In that first meeting over several cocktails, I felt an immediate connection with him. He had a hard luck story which he shared with me and we connected on an emotional level that I had never experienced with my husband. Things heated up between us and within a few weeks, I knew I had fallen for him.

I remember the terrible day when I had to tell the truth to my husband, it was heart-wrenching because I still cared for him. I did hurt him and myself in the process. I later apologized to him, and I truly was sorry to have caused him pain. I didn't grieve properly for the end of my marriage and fell in love right away with another man. I felt like I finally found my soul mate who understood my deepest feelings and he would cuddle me and tell me everything was all right.

We were two wounded hedonists in love. The relationship was like the *Titanic*, a ship heading for an iceberg without a captain at the helm. Neither one of us wanted to be in control, at least my husband had some control, but for my English boyfriend and me, it was a free-for-all. We'd party hard every weekend, exploring the Sydney nightlife.

Then came a period of extreme loss; I lost my job and the relationship with my boyfriend ran its course after three and a half years. We had to move out of our apartment and I no longer had a car. Little did I know at the time, this was the best thing that could have happened to me. When you don't take care of a situation, the Universe takes care of it for you! I didn't know what to do. I had no money to fly home and I was ashamed to tell my parents of my failure, plus I was deeply depressed and lacked sound judgment. That is when my boyfriend suggested I go live on the Central Coast with his friend for a while and that's where the healing began.

Chapter Five - My first Vibrational Healing Session

"When we come close to those things that break us down, we touch those things that also break us open. And in that breaking open, we uncover our true nature.

~Wayne Muller

After my breakup with my boyfriend, I lived up the Central Coast of Australia in a little town called Umina, just North of Sydney with a gay couple and their dogs at their weekend home. Tom was the accountant for my boyfriend's dotcom agency and he had talked Tom into taking me in as I had no place else to go. They graciously took me in for a while and I slept in their converted garage.

I had all my belongings, a bike, a bed, my clothes and personal effects and two dogs. It was a top spot, three blocks back from the beach and the backyard was private and lush with beautiful Australian native flowers and trees. I had just broken up with my boyfriend and was a physical & emotional wreck. The hedonistic and abusive relationship had taken its toll on me. I was grieving for both relationships, the end of my marriage three and a half years prior and this one. I had been on dexamphetamines, pills I was prescribed for my ADHD. I had also been partying hard with drinking and drugs, drinking tons of coffee and eating a terrible diet. I was thin, pale, with big bags under my eyes and extremely depressed. Needless to say, I was pretty damaged.

It was January of 2001, and I had lost my job three months prior, and had been unemployed and depressed. My heart was broken by the breakup with my boyfriend; I was in it for the long run and was devastated when he ended things. I put up with so much emotional abuse because I loved him. I had learned as a child that emotional abuse and love went hand in hand. So there I was, thousands of miles from my family, living with an acquaintance, unemployed, with very little money, no friends and feeling shattered into thousands of pieces. It was very scary.

I realized I had no idea who I was, I had jumped from boyfriend to boyfriend to husband to boyfriend and I never learned who Beth was. This was a sad realization at the age of thirty five. All I had wanted in my life was to have fun, travel, learn and be loved, those were my only goals. I really never held any ambitions; I was very naïve and child-like for a long time.

The stark reality of the situation demanded that I get serious, quit drinking and doing drugs; I even stopped sugar, dairy and wheat cold turkey. I was still smoking cigarettes, but planned to quit them as well. I was smoking what the Aussies called "rollies", or roll your owns. A bag of tobacco and rolling papers lasted a long time, a few weeks, which was a lot longer than buying them in a box. I had just enough money to buy food each day and ate sparingly.

It was hell as my body went through detox from the alcohol, drugs and sugar, all at the same time. The extreme depression and fear I felt was intense, I cried on and off throughout the day. I started running two hours a day down the beach. Nature gave me the only joy I had during those times. I was replenished by the beauty of the beaches, the sunlight on the water, the nurturing trees and flowers that grew in the back yard and sharing my life with my two beautiful dogs. The salt water cleansed my body and the sun nourished my soul.

My daily routine went something like this, I rose at 6 a.m., did yoga poses, ran for an hour down the beach with the dogs, swam, ate breakfast, cried, meditated, searched on Tom's computer for jobs, ate lunch, cried, took the dogs down to the beach for a run and swim, sent out resume's and employment letters, afternoon rest and cry, dinner with Tom and bedtime with a cry before sleep.

I knew my time was limited living there and that I had to find work soon. Tom made it clear that I needed to move out as soon as I found a job. This incentive really got me in gear, if Tom hadn't laid down the ground rules, I may have wallowed in my misery for many more months.

At one point when I broke down in pre-menstrual, detoxing rage and tears, he just looked at me shaking his head with compassion and exclaimed, "Honey, you need your mother." He was right, I did need my mother, but by God I knew I needed to work this mess out on my own as I had certainly dug the ditch deep enough myself and crawled right into it. It was my duty to find a way out on my own.

After two and a half months of detoxing, eating right, exercising, meditation and yoga, I began to look and feel better. I had developed a stronger physique and my eyes were bright, the bags underneath had vanished, my tongue was pink instead of brownish white and my face had a fresh glow again. I had mental clarity and my emotions were calmer although there was still so much work I had to do in understanding myself. This was the first time I had mental clarity since I was a teenager.

It was during this time that my meditations and intuition got stronger. I remember having one meditation where I left my body and entered into a state of total bliss. It was like nothing I can describe, I was completely weightless and I entered into a vast void of nothingness where everything was perfect and all I felt was love, total relaxation and a connectedness to all things.

I also started to receive messages in my meditations. On my daily run, I passed a house with a sign out the front advertising massage. I kept getting the urge to go into the house, but I didn't see the point since I couldn't afford to pay for a massage. In those days, I still did not trust the Universe enough, not allowing the Universe to give me what I needed unless it made sense logically. After a few weeks of these strong feelings, I finally went in one day to talk to the woman, Andrea. I told her I had limited funds but she said she could work with that.

I told her about my emotional devastation. She listened intently and then asked if I wanted to try energetic healing? I asked her if it was similar to Reiki and she said, "This blows Reiki out the window." Ok, I said, what did I have to lose?

I lay face down on the table while she explained she wasn't going to be touching me at all, just channeling energy into my chakras, vortices or focal points for receiving and transmitting energy through my body. As she did this I engaged in deep breathing into my whole being, I felt immense pressure in my body and I began to weep as the pressure released and my energy centers opened. I sobbed for close to an hour while she worked on me and I recall her asking me to imagine all my negative thoughts going into a pink balloon, filling it up.

Once all the negative thoughts were in there, she asked that I bring down a pair of silver scissors and cut the cord, seeing the balloon float away and leaving my mind free of negativity. When she was done with the session, I sat up, emotionally drained (literally!) and amazed by the experience.

We spoke and she said that she knew I was an indigo child, and had the power and wisdom to use my guides to help me create a beautiful life and she then asked why had I not done this to manifest a wonderful existence here on earth? Why was I not using my power? I couldn't answer her. I had forgotten who I was. I had forgotten that I was a beloved child of God and always had help from the other side. I had forgotten what it was to be powerful. I had been giving my power away all these years to the men in my life, in exchange for love. I had been looking for love outside of myself all of my life. I was never taught, like so many others, how to love myself.

After I walked out of her house I felt an enormous difference in my body, I felt no pain at all! All of my little aches and pains were gone! I felt grounded and connected to the earth for the first time in my entire life. The colors around me were enhanced and everything seemed electric. It reminded me of being on magic mushrooms, yet there were no drugs in my system. This was a true state of being, a natural state. I felt like the light being that I was, I felt joyous, like I was inside a dream, floating and free. It was truly a miraculous feeling, how could this be and what did she do?

For the rest of the day I danced around with glee, floating elatedly in this new found bliss. I played in the water which felt like pure heaven caressing me; I laughed with my dogs and smiled at the flowers, which seemed to smile back at me. I was seeing through the eyes of love. I walked along the beach and felt a profound sense of belonging to this planet and a deep oneness with all things, a joyful and pure connectedness to all that was. It was a dreamy state of being. I finally knew what happiness felt like. I finally felt like I belonged.

I knew that I had to learn what this energy healing was all about so that I could help others feel this way and keep my own energy clear. This was so profound to me that I went back to Andrea to tell her of my experience and ask her where I could learn energetic healing. Within two months I was studying at the school in Sydney.

The blissful feeling lasted about three days and then my emotional pain started to creep back in. It was then I realized that I would have to work to clear my baggage, change my thinking, behavior and lifestyle in order to reach this natural state of bliss in my daily life. It was my years of conditioning that had set up negative patterns which created blocks in my thinking and consequently in my life.

We create what we think. I had learned from a young age to think critically and judgmentally and even be paranoid from my mother. I don't blame my Mom, but even in the afterlife, she has told me that she truly believed that her own life was difficult and therefore, it was. In the place where she is now, she sees that her own misaligned beliefs were the source of her unhappiness, not her external circumstances. I'm grateful that I have been able to grow beyond what I was taught and that I connected with the truth.

I spent three months on the Central Coast and then landed a job at a TV station in Sydney, where I was the Executive Assistant for some of the top Executives who ran the station. The job paid well, but I felt like a fish out of water because the TV industry is cut throat, it's all about making money and appearance. I would sit in meetings and listen to the Executives discuss the talent as if they were commodities. There was no concern for the soul, spirit or even the feelings of the people they hired, it was about ratings and money and the bottom line. Often after working on a

TV show for ten years, a presenter would be let go simply because of their age and looks. I saw a lot of people get hurt and the general culture was one of fear.

At the same time I was working at the TV station, I was enrolled in my Higher Self Connection Course for two years at the Australian Academy of Applied Parapsychology. Every Tuesday night I would go to class with fourteen students and a wonderful teacher. I learned to meditate with the intention to reconnect with my Higher Self. I loved this class! Finally, I had found a place that spoke the same language as me. We were learning all sorts of wonderful things about communicating with guides, angels, channeling energy, crystals, clearing entities and all things metaphysical. It was the only thing that kept me going while I worked at the station. The class was the real world to me, versus the world of illusion I worked in. I was beginning to connect with and grow my true self and it felt wonderful.

I'll never forget the first time I got real "proof" that what I was doing was real, that ethereal beings existed. I had been working at the TV station for about a year and a half and my friend was making a short film for Trop-Fest, a film festival held for amateurs in Sydney each year. I was in the second year of my Higher Self Connection course and in one class we had learned how to clear negative entities out of people's homes and bodies.

I was working as a Production Assistant for my friend who was the Director. On that particular day of filming, we were shooting scenes in an S & M (Sadomasochism) parlor in downtown Sydney, starting at 7am on a Sunday. While the scene was being shot in a small room upstairs, the rest of the crew, including myself, the make-up girl, hair stylist and other production assistants were waiting downstairs with "Mistress Jane" who was kindly showing us around the parlor and explaining to us exactly what went on inside.

Sadomasochism is basically where men pay to be beaten with whips and props in a role playing environment by women; dominatrix's, or mistress's and they derive immense sexual pleasure from this act. There is a lot of dark, negative energy created by these activities. While Mistress Jane was demonstrating different spanking methods, she told us how the room we were in had a dark spirit, or entity that liked to knock pictures off the wall and was known for other mischievous acts around the place. Right at that exact moment, the makeup girl said that she felt something heavy on her chest and she looked very distressed and reported she was having difficulty breathing. I didn't have time to think, I just knew this entity we were speaking of was trying to crawl into her. I told her to come with me into the other room quickly and grabbed her by the arm, leading the way. I stood across from her, called upon my Higher Self and the Guardians of Light to join me. Together, we created a column of white light energy next to her going up to the Universe.

I channeled white light onto her and commanded the Guardians of Light to draw this negative energy out of her body and into the white light to be taken to the place in the astral plane where it belonged. I channeled the light for a couple of minutes and then I felt a tingling down my arm and out my hand. Right at that moment she said she felt a tingling in her chest and a moment later she said that the pressure was gone. I then sealed the area and thanked my Higher Self and Guardians of Light, releasing them with loving gratitude. The girl and I looked at each other and I declared, it's over, it's gone. We then hugged each other with great joy and relief.

I remember while all of this was going on the rest of the crew looking at us as if we were from another planet, wondering what the hell had just happened, but this girl and I knew exactly what went down, we both felt it. The tingling down my arm reminded me of the stars in those animated films that come out of wands of wizards and fairy godmothers. Later, she came to me, thanked me again, and asked me where I learned how to do that. I told her about my course. She was amazed, as was I; it was real proof that what I was learning was real and that I could have a positive effect in helping others in this strange world of the unseen.

After I graduated from the Higher Self Connection course, I did not have the self esteem or confidence yet to find work or create an existence based on what I had learned. I knew what I wanted, but I didn't know how to get there. I was full of doubt. I was still relying on the patriarchal, material world to define my life. I left the TV station and worked in temp jobs here and there and I still felt lost and unsatisfied. Although I had reconnected to my Higher Self, I had not undergone a deep healing, I had not let go of all of my past and the guilt, sadness, shame and remorse that was attached to it. I had not forgiven myself. It was at this time

my mother passed away unexpectedly.

Chapter Six - Out of the Ashes

"So long as we believe in our heart of hearts that our capacity is limited and we grow anxious and unhappy, we are lacking in faith. One who truly trusts in God has no right to be anxious about anything."

~Paramahansa Yogananda

Following my mother's death, I returned to the United States to live with my sister in upstate New York. During this time I met an amazing therapist who helped me heal on a very deep level. She worked with me for many months helping me to come to terms with my past, forgive myself and accept what had happened and move forward. I remember clearly after a profound session that I felt like I had been charged with electricity, I felt totally amped up with this heightened feeling, like a hundred pounds had been lifted off of me and surge of energy was running through my body. This elated feeling lasted a couple of weeks. I had cleared a lot of old baggage out of my being. My self esteem was growing stronger daily and my confidence was building.

I was working at another job that I didn't like, in a subservient role that left me feeling undervalued. I needed to do something that came from my heart, to help others. I have the personality to be a leader, not a follower so it's important that I have my own business. That's when the Universe stepped in to help.

I had been doing the Vibrational healing on friends for a few years but was lacking the courage to turn it into a real business. In my boss' office there was this globe filled with water and a golf tee and a golf ball. The goal was to get the golf ball to land on the tee and stay there. I would play with the toy while I was in my boss' office, if she were on the phone but I never got the golf ball to land on the tee, it was seemingly impossible.

I was feeling like it was time to leave that company and start my own business more and more, yet I was scared to leave the security of a weekly paycheck. One day while my boss was out, I went into her office and picked up the golf ball globe and asked my guides, "Guides, if this is the right time to leave and start my own business, make this golf ball land on the tee." On my first try, there it went, the golf ball floated effortlessly up in the water and landed perfectly on the tee. It was one of those eerie moments when time just stands still and I felt completely connected to all things. I just stood there staring in disbelief at this toy, and I knew that my guides were saying, "YES, go jump off the cliff and we will catch you!!"

I was so happy and I felt so supported and loved in that moment. A few days went by and I began to doubt that what had happened was real. So I went back to the golf toy and I asked the same question and again on my third try, the ball landed on the tee. Well, now this was, without a shadow of a doubt a very big sign confirming that indeed it was time to leave. For eight months I had played with that toy and never landed the ball on the tee, and then twice in one week after asking this question, the ball landed on the tee, coincidence? I think not!

I decided to call my business Spirit Works, because I had seen how Spirit had worked in my own life and I wanted to help others to see that they could live their life from a spiritual perspective and create a dream life by trusting in Spirit, in God. Starting my own business was one of the best decisions I have ever made in my life. I get to live my purpose every single day. For twenty five years I had longed to know what my purpose was. It got to the point that I wanted to tear my hair out in desperation of finding out what I was meant to be doing. I wanted to measure up to my father's work in helping feed the planet and do something truly helpful for the people on this earth.

I see now that the early chaos in my family, my mother's mental illness and my own struggle growing up was all part of the bigger picture in my life's purpose. I went to the depths of despair in my self-abuse. Now I have compassion and understanding for other's pain which I can use in my work. When I see someone hurting themselves, instead of judging them, I just know that they're in a lot of pain and deserve my compassion. I know that their behavior can change with love and encouragement from themselves and others and their connection to their Higher Self.

If my life had been easy and perfect, I never would have had the understanding of the pain people go through. I am so grateful for all my life experiences, even though it was incredibly difficult at the time.

I believe we are all wounded in some way and it is up to us to overcome that in our lifetime and heal the wounds. What are the other alternatives, to stay wounded or to become more wounded...no thanks! God put a key of truth in each and every one of us and it is up to us to search for it. It's important to ask others for help. We aren't meant to do it alone. Everyone's journey on this earth is highly personal, what works for one person may not work for another and we have to respect that individual's path even if it doesn't seem right to us.

Before my mother passed away she and my father came out to Australia to visit me. I'm so glad they did because it was the last time I saw her alive. When they saw the life I lived, they became aware that I was sick, physically, emotionally and spiritually. I had hidden everything from them which was easy to do since I lived on the other side of the world. They never heard my pain and anguish through the telephone lines as I would only call them when I was feeling great. When they saw the truth for themselves with their own eyes, they did not judge me. My mother told me what she saw, that I was living a life of an alcoholic and she said she felt that I was very sad.

She still believed in me saying that she knew one day I was going to turn my life around and be a success- even when I myself did not believe this. At this point she was very sick, but no one knew this. I remember seeing these big blood bruises on her arms, and the last person I had seen these same types of bruises on was a receptionist at a company I had worked for, who died a year before from cancer. I knew that it wouldn't be long for my Mom.

A few days later when they flew out, both of them told me that they loved me and that they had always loved me and would always love me no matter what. I truly felt unconditional love and I knew that the truth was that they had always loved me unconditionally: now I was finally able to see it. It was my own self love and worth that was lacking.

My mother died nine months later unexpectedly and it was a huge shock to the entire family. She was 70 years old and she died less than a year after her mother who was 94. My father had called me two days earlier, to tell me she had gone into a coma. She had gone into the hospital to have her lungs checked out and when they put the camera down her throat to feed into her lungs, she couldn't breathe, panicked and her heart fibrillated.

My father could not bear being at the hospital and seeing his beloved Willie with all the tubes sticking out of her, so he went home. She died the next day and he received a call from the hospital; no one was there with her when she died.

I was on the beach in Australia, it was raining, I was watching a friend surf with a towel over my head to keep the raindrops off when a black crow flew over my head and cawed. Normally seagulls are at the beach, but this day, it was the black crow that cried out in the rain. I instantly felt funny, I knew something was wrong and I headed for the car. My friend followed shortly thereafter and we drove back to my house. I changed into a black sweater and a few minutes later my sister called and told me mom had died. Just like that!

One day she was alive, the next day in a coma and the day after that, dead. I was devastated. I journeyed 46 hours back to Arkansas for the funeral. A black crow was waiting at Tokyo airport where I had a nine hour layover. It watched me from the airport window when I fell asleep on the floor and was there when I woke up.

It wouldn't be an exaggeration to say I cried every day for two years over my mother's death. There was so much sadness and regret inside of me! I have finally healed this part of me. My mom was a truly amazing woman, but she never felt that about herself. She never saw what a wonderful human being she was and she suffered under the illusion that she wasn't smart enough or rich enough or accomplished enough or pretty enough. She was all those things and more. She was a beautiful soul and dearly loved. She gave me my love of song and dance and all sports. She loved spending time in nature and my love of the great outdoors came from her. She taught me to be open and enjoy the fun times in life without regret. She shared with me the joy of cooking and art. She had so many wonderful gifts and was truly a beautiful soul.

My father went downhill after my mother's death. He began to drink more and he isolated himself in his house with his books. He lost interest in life. A year following her death he had a pacemaker implanted, his heart too, was tired. Three years later, his body started to shut down and his friends called to tell us that dad really was not well and needed serious attention, which my dad would not divulge to us himself.

We took turns looking after him. When it was my turn, I flew down to take care of dad while he was in the hospital trying to determine what his illness was. It was an eleven day stretch. I quizzed the doctors daily, taking pages of notes with what they told me and waited, with daily phone calls updating my siblings and his friends. I remember announcing to him that 4:00 pm was "cuddle time" and I would lie next to him on the hospital bed and hold him. It dawned on me that he probably hadn't been held in three years and he seemed to appreciate the nurturing. It was good for me too. It was during this time that I realized that I had misunderstood my father for my entire life. I was now beginning to understand why he acted the way he did. He had been mistreated as a child and never got over it. The truth was being revealed to me and it gave me a whole new perspective on my life. I was able to view him with a great deal of compassion and love as I saw that he had only ever done the best that he could.

Somewhere around day nine, things got intense; dad was getting tired of being woken up in the middle of the night and being poked with needles. He was irritable, I was frustrated by the lack of answers, it seemed the tests were going on and on and nothing concrete was being discovered. Plus, Hurricane Ike came through town and caused a lot of damage. I had to sleep in a hotel that night because it wasn't safe to drive home. I was so stressed and tired and I began to lose my composure - which doesn't really seem the right word for it. I think sanity may be the right word, yes, it felt like my whole world was being turned upside down.

Two days later, a young doctor told me that dad would need to go into hospice care. I had to ask him what hospice meant as I was not familiar with that word at the time. He stammered while trying to explain that there was nothing more they could do. He couldn't tell me how long it would be before he died, not even a suggestion, which is fair-enough, because everyone's experience is different. So that was it...the diagnoses was terminally ill.

I remember when the doctor told him to his face that he had to go into hospice; Dad didn't understand what he was being told. He couldn't grasp that nothing more could be done, that this was the end. I had to spell it out for him. Once he understood, he grew very quiet and retreated to a place deep within. It was a terribly painful moment for both of us.

I took him home to his house and nursed him. One night he requested I read *The Raven,* to him, by Edgar Allen Poe. Whenever I read the verse "and never more" in reference to the beloved departed Lenore, my father chimed in, only when he spoke his words, we both knew they were meant for my mother. It was clear he missed his wife greatly. I remember telling him that mom would be there to greet him on the other side when he died, and that his young baby son and brother would be there too. He didn't believe me.

He died two months after leaving the hospital, in his home, which was his wish. My sister and I stood at the end of his bed and watched his life force leaving his body the day he died, exactly a year ago today as I sit writing this. He is free and at peace. I have had readings with a medium since his death and he told me that I was right, that mom was there to greet him that he hadn't believed me but that she was there, much to his delight. He also shared with me from the other side that he recognized that he hadn't been present with us as children and that he regretted his behavior. He said he would have done it differently if he had to do it over again and told me to follow my heart.

My father was a truly great man. He too had a beautiful soul and he gave me my love of the English language, love of science and nature and taught me to be a free thinker. We shared a love of travel and other cultures and he taught me that all men, women and children deserve to be treated with fairness and respect. He also taught me the importance of honesty which I didn't apply to my life until after my awakening. Being honest with yourself is the most important rule to follow.

I was happy he got to see the real me before he died, he saw me becoming whole and healing. I spent my entire life trying to be someone I thought my father would be proud of and failed miserably. I worked in the media in jobs I hated because they were in the mainstream and paid well. Ironically enough, it was only when I began to expand my true self (the girl who loved oils, crystals, angels and was intuitive and sensitive to what other's felt) that my father began to be proud of me. It was because he felt my happiness. Dad could hear the excitement in my voice on the other end of the phone when I talked about my life. He was proud when I mustered the courage to start my own business. It was then that I realized that all he ever wanted was for me to be happy and that it was me who had put all those self-imposed restrictions upon myself.

I still have issues I am working on and always will, I believe that's part of this human experience. I don't claim to be perfect but I am always striving to improve myself. Now, I accept and love myself even on the tough days. I am always working to love myself better. I have compassion for myself no matter what I'm going through. Mostly it's my attitude that is completely different.

I wake up grateful and I look forward to creating my future. I have confidence and good self-esteem. My self-talk has completely changed; I encourage myself with loving words instead of criticizing and judging myself. Every time I do a healing on someone, it helps me to heal in some way. It's a total win-win situation.

The pure act of helping others, of living my life in service to God is the most powerful medicine that I could ever receive. The feeling of gratitude I get every time I do my work is so strong it brings tears of joy to my eyes and fills my heart. I believe that when you do finally take the plunge and live your dream that the

Universe rewards you. In other words, when you find the courage to jump off the cliff, either the net catches you or you learn to fly.

Once you live your life doing what you are supposed to be doing, life becomes the way it should be, purposeful, meaningful and joyous. Confucius was right, "If you enjoy what you do, you will never work another day in your life." There will always be issues to work through, aspects of myself to improve and problems to solve but I am blessed and I know that I am loved, loving and loveable. I am whole, I am healed and I am eternally grateful for my life.

Chapter Seven - Surrendering to the Light

"I let go of a broken heart, I let go to an open heart, I let go of my broken dreams, I let go to the mystery and I believe in the miracles, I believe in the spiritual, I believe in the One above, I believe in the one I love."

~Michael Franti

The date was August 2, 2009, I had just returned from a wonderful, mystical month-long spiritual journey in Southern India, a year following my father's passing. That was my fourth trip to India, my country of birth, and there have been many changes since I last visited there 23 years ago. The sights, smells and sounds remain the same; the women dressed in layers of beautiful, rich fabrics, wearing jasmine garlands in their long black hair, the sidewalks bustling with vendors selling fresh mango, papaya, and sandalwood oil; the traffic of motorcycles, bicycles carrying a family of five, rickshaws, cows and cars all following a path of near collision but somehow everyone making it safely to their destination; the numerous temples with statues of many Gods with the orange, pink and red pastes and ash for

the forehead and devotional chants playing in the background...
ahhh, yes, there is only one India.

Interestingly enough, I hadn't planned to go to India; it was never
on my agenda. It was, however, the divine's plan that I go. It
came about when a friend mentioned that there was a women's
retreat organized from Syracuse, New York at an Ayurvedic clinic
in Trivandrum. I was interested in undergoing pancha karma,
which is the classic Ayurvedic regimen for purifying and
rejuvenating the physical and emotional bodies using herbal
medicines and various treatments such as daily herbal oil baths.
Originally designed to bolster the health and longevity of royalty,
Pancha Karma is a process designed to "hit the reset button" in
our health and lives.

It's inexpensive to stay in India; the main cost was the airfare, so
it only made sense that I stay longer. Within two months of
hearing about the trip I was on a plane to India. This is how the
Universe works when you surrender to the Divine's plan.

The pancha karma was challenging, the internal and external
medicines working to expel the toxins deep from within me. The

manager at the clinic explained that the process was like the goddess (Devi) stirring the waters of the sea with a giant stick, bringing up all the sediment that had formed on the bottom, so that at the time of expulsion the sea could be fully cleansed once again.

On the sixth day I felt weak and exhausted, but our group's motto, "Bash on regardless" taken from a sign at a nearby military base, helped me to soldier on through the rough part. I so enjoyed and appreciated the four women (goddesses) with me on the retreat and am so happy to have had the chance to know them and create a strong bond for support in my life. We got along famously, helped each other with laughter and shared stories and by being there for each other. Along with the pancha karma there were many activities organized for us including a hike up Medicine mountain, a trip to Kanyakumari on the tip of the Southern coast, incense making, mehendi or decoration of the hands and feet using henna, a violin and drum concert, mandala making using flower petals, puja and yoga and meditation every morning.

I came out the other side feeling pure, clear and rejuvenated. I was told I would continue to feel the effects for months to come and it would forever alter the course of my health, which I believe to be true.

At Sai Baba's ashram, I shared a room with seven women from all over the world: Japan, Poland, Russia, India and Germany. I performed daily seva (selfless service) at the Western canteen, serving food without pay. Sai Baba believed that selfless service purifies the heart. I studied, prayed, meditated, chanted and spread the light.

At the ashram, there was one day when I was sitting in Darshan, which is Sanskrit for "auspicious viewing". It is the temple where Sai Baba makes his appearances and shines his light upon all of the seekers who gather before him. I was heady with the pure sensory beauty of the smell of jasmine, the rhythmic chanting and the silk sari's surrounding me. With my eyes closed, I psychically tuned into Sai Baba's energy, which felt like the rays of the sun, a golden liquid light permeating my very being. An hour or so into the session, I rose, a single figure in the sea of bodies and made my way out of the temple, feeling guided by His energy. I began to walk back to the dormitories, but turned into an open field. The sky was completely overcast except for one small eye-shaped hole in the dark clouds. I stood there, my eyes fixated on the open hole and watched in awe as the sun moved directly into that open space, creating a Golden Eye, watching me. I knew at that moment that Sai Baba had blessed me and I felt free and connected to my God Self.

I felt a clear understanding that I was on the right path, and continued daily discipline and devotion is needed to reach the higher planes to support my life's mission. I left Puttaparthi with Baba's mottos, "Help Ever, Hurt Never" and "Love All, Serve All" secured in my heart and happy that this man/divine being exists to help those who need him.

What I experienced on this journey was a deepening of my commitment to living a life aligned with the Truth of the Divine within me. I want this (my) life to be great, not mediocre, not ordinary, but great. I want to share my wisdom with others and help them align with their Truth. I do this in my work by delivering the light (jyothi), the love (prema), the truth (sathya) in the form of Vibrational healing. I'm on a mission from God (and it does not involve $50, a pair of sunglasses and a case of beer like the Blues Brothers).

My desire is to help others in their growth, expansion and self awareness so that they may align with their divine selves. I believe much of our suffering comes about because we align with the ego personality of the human being rather than the divine within. The light dispels negativity and supports transformation. I want to know peace within my heart and truly be of service to others to allow them to seek their own truth.

My goal with this trip was to purify the body and to bring in more light, raising my vibration so that I can continually be aligned with my Divine Self. Creating a great life takes dedication and commitment and a whole lot of love and compassion for oneself. I feel blessed and grateful and happy that I am exactly where I am supposed to be and doing exactly what I need to be doing. I am given opportunities like this one by the Universe to strengthen my faith. I am living in the flow, a feeling one gets when they have surrendered their life to the divine. In this moment, I feel peace and love in my heart and this brings me great joy. My wish is for everyone to feel this way, and so I send my love and blessings to every one of you.

The Way of the Yogini

About a year after returning from India I received another message from Spirit. I was in the grocery store one night shopping for food and I passed a magazine rack in the health section. There on the shelf was "Yoga" magazine. I had passed this same rack many times before but this time, a feeling came over me that was very strong that I was to buy the Yoga magazine. Okay, I said to Spirit, I will get it. I took it home and flipped through it and nothing really caught my eye so I put it aside. About 3 weeks later, I flipped through it again and this time an advertisement for Sivananda Yoga Teacher's Training in the Bahamas jumped out at me. There was something vaguely familiar about the ad. Then I realized that when I had made my vision board a year or so before, I had cut out a picture of a woman on a beautiful white sand beach, her arms stretched out wide, with a caption above saying, "Expand Your Horizons". It was the very same advertisement! Immediately I knew I was to do the yoga teacher's certification course beginning December

1ˢᵗ, 2010, about 6 months away. That night I signed up for the month long, 200 hour intensive.

Even though I had only been practicing yoga for one year, I knew that it was my destiny to teach this discipline. It incorporated all · of the principles that Spirit had taught me on my journey were essential to good health in order to live a spiritual life and grow my Divine Self. Yoga incorporates proper diet, proper breathing, poses, meditation and positive thinking, all of the elements I use to counsel others in my sessions. The yogic philosophy also teaches us how to be a good human being in this world by following a practice of compassion for all things in the form of non violence, non-stealing, truthfulness, peacefulness, focus and concentration, meditation, poses, breath control, controlling the senses, practicing contentment, self-study, study of the scriptures, moderation in all things and living a pure life devoted to God.

Yoga camp, as it was called, was quite an experience that I loved. Forty five students from all over the world convened at the Sivananda Ashram to undertake this challenge. The yoga teacher's training was started by Swami Vishnu-Devananda in

1961 in Canada and 50 years later, the Sivananda organization is responsible for accrediting almost 27,000 yoga teachers worldwide. No easy feat, I promise you. Swami Vishnu-Devananda was a direct disciple of Swami Sivananda, a living teacher who served selflessly to thousands firstly as a doctor and then later as a spiritual leader. He founded the Divine Life Society in 1936 and then The Yoga Vedanta Forest Academy in 1948 to disseminate spiritual knowledge and train people in Yoga and Vedanta to help people become strong and healthy in body and mind and evolve spiritually.

Swami Sivananda's teachings combined all paths of yoga into one, The Yoga of Synthesis and his motto was, "Serve, Love, Give, Purify, Meditate, Realize". The ashram is a beautiful piece of land with water on both sides and six outdoor yoga platforms, a kitchen, dining area, a temple, showers and bathrooms, a boutique and one of the most beautiful white sand beaches with turquoise waters that I have ever seen. The weather was an added challenge to our daily schedule; we had 3 cold snaps that lasted a few days each which blew down from the North that saw us practicing yoga in down jackets and blankets brrrr. Then the wind would blow from the South and we would be blessed with

80 degree sunny days and everyone would relax and smile again.

Little did most of the students realize what they had signed up for! The schedule was rigorous with a 5:30am wake up bell and satsang (a gathering of spiritual aspirants) which involved meditation in the temple at 6am each morning as well as chanting and a lecture, followed by two hours of yoga, then our first vegetarian meal of the day at 10am, a noon class of either chanting or teachings of the Bhagavad Gita, which means (Songs of God) then an hour break followed by two hours of either Vedantic Philosophy or Anatomy classes, another two hour yoga class where we learned to teach, our evening meal at 6pm, an hour of karma yoga and then back to the temple for Satsang with either a lecture or performance from some of the top teachers and performers in the world, and finally bedtime at 10:30pm. I slept like a rock. We had Saturdays off but were still required to attend satsang and karma yoga. Karma yoga is selfless service, where you carry out a duty with no expectation of reward. The ashram has a list of daily tasks that need to happen in order for everyone's needs to be taken care of such as cooking, washing dishes, trash duty, setting up the temple, etc.

Karma yoga acts to purify your heart as you work for the highest good of all without any pay or thought of reward for just yourself.

By the second week, we were given so much information that it became difficult to process with our time limitation. The whole point of doing yoga is to have the realization that our very essence is God and that we are not separate from God. All of the poses (Asanas), breathwork (Pranayama), purification and vegetarian diet, relaxation, study of scriptures, prayer and meditation is designed to control the body and mind to allow the Divine Self to emerge. One must be vigilant in one's daily practice in order to be a yogi or yogini. It takes commitment and dedication, and an understanding that spiritual evolution is the main goal. A true yogi has to renounce worldly desires, all the pleasures of the senses. We were given examples of this by the monks that lived and taught at the ashram whose daily sadhana (spiritual practice) is constant and true. As Sivananda would say, "a yogi should be in the world, but not of the world."

Our training was hard work and the difficulty could be felt by each student who struggled with one or more or all aspects of the course. It is designed to be hard for a reason, for a yogi knows

91

when you just satisfy your sense desires, that which you desire can never be truly satisfied and your nectar turns into poison. It is the product of hard work and discipline, turning your senses inward, that creates spiritual liberation. So what initially appears to be poison in the form of hard work ultimately becomes the nectar, freedom from desire.

I loved the community, I loved being around all these beautiful people with all their different backgrounds, personalities and issues and humor. I honor them and thank them for being my teachers. I learned that in order to be a great human being that I need to overcome my own personal preferences, my likes and dislikes and honor every soul that I meet and treat them as I wish to be treated. I loved living in nature, even when the wind wouldn't stop blowing; I loved feeling connected to Mother Earth's heart beat. On a good day, the water was sublime. I had one of the best Christmas and New Year's celebration ever at the ashram, surrounded by my fellow students; with our hearts open enjoying each other, the music and the atmosphere. I loved learning; my mind was stimulated with interesting topics every day. I loved pushing the body with the breath work and poses every day for a month. I loved this experience, with all its challenges and blessings.

I am so grateful to have this knowledge and I want nothing more than to share it with others so they too can grow. I recognize that as a yoga teacher, there may not be many students who wish to be yogis and renounce all worldly pleasures. But I think it's important to start by helping people find the stillness within and become centered. If there is peace within our hearts, then peace can grow in the community, then the country and the world. Each of us is responsible for creating a lifestyle that harbors that peace and Yoga is a path that can lead us there.

I left the ashram with a stronger Yoga practice, another wonderful experience, many great connections and a certificate that allows me to teach yoga to others.

Powers of Manifestation

I lived in upstate New York for five and a half years. Living there was a challenge for me as I felt the dense energy, as if someone was sitting on my head. In the winter time the sun disappears for a few months and the whole town turns one shade of grey. I have lived in some of the most beautiful and light-filled places on earth, so that was a new experience for me. I moved to New York to reconnect with my family, to purify and heal on many levels and to build my reservoir of light. That means, raising my vibration and holding a large amount of light with which to help others raise their vibration and seek the light. I was sent there to shine my light and I obeyed the call to duty until it was finally time to move on.

It was in New York that I began to learn to consciously manifest. I had purified my body and raised my vibration to the point where I could ask for something and then the Universe would bring it to me. Manifestation is when our creative thought forms actualize in the physical plane. I had manifested what I needed before but this was different because now I was becoming consciously aware of how to do it. The first time I did this I asked God for an i-pod. It was a fairly new gadget on the market and I didn't want to buy a cd player, because I could see that MP3 music was taking over so I needed an i-pod and I didn't have a lot of money so I asked to receive one.

About a week later a friend at work had been gifted an i-pod which she said she didn't want because she didn't have time as she had four children and a busy job, so she passed it onto me. I was so grateful and thanked God for granting my wish.

About one week later I was in my favorite park walking my dog with a friend of mine. When we finished walking and returned to the car I looked down on the ground and saw an i-pod with headphones lying there. I picked it up and saw that it was an 80g i-pod. I took it home and looked on the machine to try and find the owner and made some phone calls, looked up his name in the phone book and also googled him but could not locate him. I also checked the lost ads on Craig's List and in the paper. I figured he must have been visiting from out of town so I kept the i-pod and realized it was a gift from God. There were over 7,000 songs on the i-pod and I was thrilled to receive it and five years later am still thrilled. In some ways that i-pod changed my life.

A week later I was in the same park at night and was driving home when I saw another i-pod on the ground. A week later, I was walking in the woods and found another i-pod. In one month

I had four i-pods, I found three and was given one. I gave two away. I was absolutely incredulous at God's generosity.

Another time, right after my camera died, I asked around to find out what was the best little digital camera on the market. A friend told me that she loved her Canon Powershot. I spent some time checking it out online and then looked up into the air and said, "Ok Angels, I need a Canon Powershot!" I then left to go on a walk with my dog. I began my usual route and then thought to myself, I had better go to the bathroom first, so I reversed directions and headed toward the restrooms and I passed a bench and there on the bench was a camera in a case. The park was crowded so I picked up the camera and asked the nearest person if it was theirs and they said no. So I unzipped the case and lo and behold, inside was a Canon Powershot! Within half an hour of asking I received exactly what I asked for. I was blown away by the Universe. This time, I knew of the park office and handed the camera in to lost and found.

True manifestation is not about finding technological gadgets or filling your life with "things", this is not the point. These experiences happened to show me that I can manifest what I desire, and to manifest what God desires for myself and others so I can be in service and live a good, honest life from a place of Love.

Moving West

The time finally came for me to make my move to the West and so I moved to Santa Fe, New Mexico on June 1, 2011. The move was extremely stressful but I was so happy to be out in place where the sun shines every day and the earth holds the powerful vibration of the crystals lying beneath the ground. I had wanted to be in a place of like-minded people near the mountains and my family and Santa Fe met all of my requirements for a place to settle and build a new life.

Shortly after moving to Santa Fe I reconnected with a woman whom I had met at the yoga ashram who was teaching Sivananda yoga in town. She was moving to Sydney, Australia and asked me if I wanted to take over her class. I applied and got the job and started teaching yoga right away. How lucky I was to walk into a town full of yoga teachers and studios and get a job teaching right away. I could feel Santa Fe wanted me to be there.

I begin each yoga class by connecting everyone to their Higher Self in a short, guided meditation invoking light into the energy field. My mission is already beginning to unfold.

I moved into a two bedroom townhome 20 minutes from town and set up my second bedroom as my healing space just as I had done in New York. But Santa Fe proved to be very different, the market was saturated with healers and I was not getting any calls from new clients even with an ad in the local paper and my flyers distributed around town. I realized that I would have to do things differently in this town.

One night I found myself in front of the statue of Our Lady of Guadalupe located at her Chapel on North Guadalupe Street. My friend Kat was with me and I prayed to her asking for help to do our healing in this town, to service the people of Santa Fe and those who visited this beautiful city, whose name means Holy Faith. I asked Our Lady of Guadalupe from my heart and thanked her in advance for her help.

A few days later I was in between appointments and was wandering around downtown near the plaza. I stumbled into this little store on Galisteo Street and found myself surrounded by metaphysical books and angel deck cards, all the stuff I loved. I asked the woman what she did there and she said she was a Hypnotist. She had a little reclining chair in the back of the small store and explained that she shut the front door when a client came in. I asked her if she did well there and she said that it was great for her because she didn't have to advertise, people just came in off the street. Then she said she was moving back to Switzerland in two weeks after being there three years. I asked her if the shop was for rent and she gave me the landlord's name and number. I thanked her and as I left her shop, I looked on the outside of the doorway and there was a picture of Our Lady of Guadalupe nailed up on the doorjamb. I stared at the picture with surety and gratitude, recognizing immediately that this was the answer to my prayer to Her. I felt totally supported in my mission and purpose and a huge feeling of joy welled up deep inside of me.

At that point, I stopped the frenetic worrying as it was clear that I would be able to manifest whatever I needed thanks to my strong connection to the Divine beings of Light who support my path.

When I called the landlord he said he could rent it to me and I struck a deal with him paying a year in advance for this little space. Within two weeks of walking into the shop, I was now the shop keeper! I had never thought of this, my very own shop, how exciting! I managed to pull everything together fairly easily and quickly. My shop, Spirit Works, www.spiritworks.me is a store front in downtown Santa Fe where I can be seen and the light can be felt by all who walk by.

At exactly the same time, my friend was moving to town and needed a place to live and since I was no longer using the second bedroom as my healing space and needed help with rent, I asked her to move in. She agreed; the Divine timing was perfect for both of us.

As a light worker, I am only just now truly learning to accept the path that I am on. It's not an easy path; it requires discipline, in what I put into my body and all my thoughts, actions and words. It is the path of complete service and devotion to God.

Since moving to New Mexico I have been challenged to stay centered and am making the appropriate adjustments to move deeper into my own divinity.

This path requires a laying down of the ego in all its forms, foregoing all excess of the pleasures the ego desires. I am not at the point yet where my personality has moved beyond the ego self, it is still very much a practice for me to think with my Divine mind or feel with my Divine heart, perhaps this will change by the time this book is published as the evolution is happening quickly.

My 20's and 30's was all about satisfying my pleasure senses and it wasn't until my 40's that I discovered that it is actually discipline and restraint, making healthy choices and helping others through God's healing work that brings me the most happiness.

I have gone from one extreme to the other. I love that I have had so many different experiences, because after having tried everything, I was able to find out what works for me and what doesn't. One of my favorite sayings is, "If you never ever go, then you never ever know."

I have been told that I'm at the point where I carry a lot of light or divine energy and my body is continually adjusting to hold this light. I hold the light best when my body is pure, when I exercise and eat really well, which means a diet that is mostly plant based and avoid processed foods, meat, caffeine, dairy, sugar and alcohol, all substances that lower my vibration. My body rejects these unhealthy choices, the divine in me is saying "no". But the ego doesn't want to die and throws a tantrum every now and again. I have no choice but to move further into the light and accept the path I am on, the path that God designated for me, the path that I chose before I came into this world.

As I fully accept and commit to this path and stop struggling against it, I can feel all the energy flowing in, supporting me on my journey. I can feel the difference and I like how it feels, so much light, so much truth and freedom. I feel that I am moving more and more into a place of serving others and doing God's work. The key is to surrender completely and trust that as a co-creator with God I will be helped and supported all along the way. As Paramahansa Yogananda says, "Self-realization is the knowing in all parts of body, mind, and soul that you are now in possession of the kingdom of God; that you do not have to pray that it come to you; that God's omnipresence is your omnipresence; and that all that you need to do is improve your knowing."

It is an understatement to say that we are living in powerful times. The energy of the planet is changing and those who don't change and wake up will suffer greatly. Old, outdated patriarchal systems are collapsing, and the return of the Divine Feminine is once again manifesting here on earth. We are being asked to treat each other and our planet with love and respect, pure and simple. We need to create sustainable systems that support the growth of the plants, ecosystems, animals and all people who live all together on this earth, regardless of race or religion. The leaders who are supporting the old system of greed will fall. We need to live in a holistic way that considers the health and happiness of all beings on this planet. The best thing that each of us can do at this time is to be healthy, raise our consciousness and act with right conduct. If everyone raises their awareness we can bring about the change in the world that needs to happen to create the golden age of Love.

I have a star hanging in my shop, I always see stars in my meditations and I understand that I am a star being. This is the kind of star that I wish to be, a luminary, a light being here to help others return to their star self. Imagine what we can do when we all tap into our Divinity; together, as stars, we can fill the world with our light.

SECTION 2- A GUIDE TO VIBRATIONAL HEALING

"The Force is what gives a Jedi his power. It's an energy field created by all living things. It surrounds us and penetrates us. It binds the galaxy together."

~Obi Wan, from *Star Wars*.

INTRODUCTION - What is Vibrational Healing?

Everything in life is energy, or vibration. Everything from a rock, a plant, an animal to a human being has a frequency at which it vibrates. The human body is made up of a series of frequencies which work in harmony when a person is healthy. When a person is unhealthy, their body's vibration alters. The nature of Vibrational healing is to help the body remember its healthy vibration or "natural" state and align the mind, the body and the soul.

The short-term result of Vibrational healing is an overall sense of well-being and an improved quality of life. The long term result is transformation to help reach one's highest potential. Therefore Vibrational healing is, in essence, transformational energy.

A person's emotional state has a great affect on the balance or imbalance of the physical body and vice versa. Our emotional body stores every experience we have ever had in our lifetime in our cells, which is known as cell imprinting. All of our experiences are stored within our cells, whether we consciously remember or not. Over the span of our lifetime, blocks in our energy systems are accumulated when negative thoughts or behavior patterns are created by our beliefs as a reaction to those events that we have experienced. These blocks need to be shifted and released to create change. When blocked, our reactions to specific situations and people or anything that triggers us, reminds us of the original event or person that created this feeling, and causes pain over and over until we uncover the source of the pain, face it, process it and let it go. These blocks lead to imbalance, which eventually can manifest into illness or disease.

Imagine that your body has a river of energy flowing through it when you are born. Throughout your life, when different experiences occur that have had a harmful effect on you, it's like a pebble is thrown into the river. If many pebbles accumulate in one area, it will result in a blockage. Vibrational energy work removes the pebbles and maintains a clear energetic system. Once you have a clear, aligned energetic system, you can fully realize your own power, and respond to life's events in a healthy way, creating a positive life based on choices that are supportive to reaching your highest potential.

A trained Vibrational energy therapist will connect with the source energy and channel it into the chakra system and subtle bodies to shift the energies within a person's auric field which kick starts their own ability to heal themselves. Human's are like self-cleaning ovens, we have, each and every one of us, the ability to heal ourselves. When we channel the light with various colors, we re-activate perfect health which is the original design of the physical body. Our body knows this; it is our ego mind that brings in the distortions, which once we start believing in, alters the perfect health of the body.

The light, (the love, the truth) is the healing agent that activates the original program for the body and the surrounding subtle bodies. It's the same as pressing the "factory reset button" on our computers, so that the default program or original design is reactivated. We must then support the energy work by shifting our beliefs and behavior to be aligned with the truth. This is the most challenging part of self-transformation. If we have any old beliefs that are based on false illusion i.e.; (I am unworthy of love), we must change this belief or the energy pattern will remain unbalanced within our energetic and physical system. Once we incorporate the new understanding of the truth into our minds, bodies and energy fields and the false illusion has been replaced, the body will no longer be affected and the disease that resulted from that false view will vanish. For example: Say a person holds the belief that all human beings are inherently bad and cancer begins to grow in their body. As long as they hold that belief, the cancer will exist. If they change their mind and now believe that human beings are beautiful and blessed and that we are privileged to be here on this earth as a living human being, the cancer will cease growing. I know that this is a strong statement and it is what I believe to be true.

You create what you think. If you think life sucks, it's going to suck. I once had a boyfriend who thought his life sucked, and guess what... it did! If you think life is beautiful, it will be beautiful - like the movie, "Life is Beautiful" directed by Roberto Benigni. The movie is about a man in the midst of the holocaust who makes his existence beautiful for his son because he believed in the beauty of life no matter what the surrounding circumstances were. Belief gives you power and you can choose to use that power to create a healthy existence or an unhealthy, unhappy one. The choice is yours.

Some people claim that to move beyond beliefs is the best way to open to one's divinity. I am not at this place yet, but I will keep my mind open to accepting this way of being if it is the best way to evolve. I can say that I am willing to continually reassess my ways of thinking and viewing myself and the world to allow for constant growth.

Chapter Eight - The Divine Energy is Available to Everyone

"We're beginning now to understand things that we know in our hearts are true but we could never measure. As we get better at understanding how little we know about the body, we begin to realize that the next big frontier in medicine is energy medicine. It's not the mechanistic part of the joints moving. It's not the chemistry of our body. It's understanding for the first time how energy influences how we feel."

~Dr. Mehmet Oz

Everything is energy. We are all comprised of energy and everything in this universe is energy...literally everything. The divine source of energy is available to every single person on this earth. It is Universal life force energy that has existed since the dawn of time, it is what created the earth, the galaxy, the Universe, it is pure creative life force.

The energy, or light is essentially pure love and it exists within and around us every second of every day. LIGHT = LOVE. It amazes me that we aren't taught that it is here for us whenever we need it and that all we have to do is tap in. What a mistake people make when they limit their beliefs! If someone believes that all of this is nonsense and that it doesn't exist, then they are effectively losing access to that part of themselves and the essential power of the Universal life force, thereby limiting their own power. Limited thinking creates a limited life. On the flip side, if you keep your mind open to all the possibilities, it's amazing what one can create, or co-create with the Universe. I believe God wants us to have an open mind and an open heart.

I call myself a sourceress, because I am connected to and working with source energy to help others access their own self-healing abilities. It is not witch-craft or black magic, it is connection to the Divine, all that is, the unlimited oneness of being, pure and simple.

The purpose of Vibrational Healing is to return us to our natural state. Our natural state is one of good health, joy, bliss, connectedness, clarity, love, and happiness. If you are overindulging in food and drink, are not exercising and feel tense and uptight most of the time, or spend too much time in your head, you are not in your natural state. When we are in our natural state, we radiate joy, are in the flow and are creative and our vibration supports our self to reach our highest potential and act in a way that is consistent with the highest good for all. Our purpose here on earth can be best realized if we are in our most natural state.

In Vibrational healing, different colors are used because each color has a different wavelength and Vibrational frequency, which affects us differently. Red has the longest wavelength and the slowest vibrational frequency, which we innately recognize as warm and stimulating. Violet has the shortest wavelength and the fastest frequency that we recognize as a cool and calming energy. We receive light and color information through our chakras, our energy centers that distribute this subtle energy to glands, organs and nerve centers throughout the body.

Since light and its colors physically affect glands and hormones, they will also have a marked influence on our moods and feelings. Science has proven that certain colors can calm the mind while others stimulate mental activity. We need light energy for nourishing our brain, our emotions and our physical body as well as our light bodies and especially our chakras. Light can also enter through our eyes, skin and our breath.

We use different colors to channel into the chakras for healing. The different colored light works at a DNA level to revitalize, heal and transmute the body's unhealthy cells, replacing them with healthy cells by using thought intent.

White	White is used to wash negativity away and to cleanse and purify the chakras. It is also the purest form of Vibrational healing as white contains all the colors.
Red	Red is a grounding color and will increase passion, enthusiasm and motivation as well as strengthen the immune system. Use this color to heal any blood or bone related diseases.
Pink	Pink helps to rebalance any chakra and is also the color used to boost self-love.
Orange	Orange stimulates joy and helps to balance the emotions. Use orange to balance the left, feminine side and right, masculine side of the body. It aids in the elimination of disease and rebuilds the immune system.
Yellow	Yellow will help rebalance and center the person and open them up to inner guidance.

	Yellow helps to banish self doubt and aids in empowerment and self belief. It is an excellent color to use in recovery from Liver, Kidney, Bladder and Gall Bladder disorders and to heal any organ that has been traumatized by deep emotions.
Green	Green is the ultimate color of healing. It is also a great color for calming and relaxing and will help a person cope with difficult emotions. Deeper shades of green will assist with sleep issues, rebuilding emotional balance and cell recovery and restoration. Lighter shades will increase fertility and creativity. Green rebalances the emotional and adrenal systems.
Blue	Blue is the best color for protection. It is a calming and peaceful color. Blue helps with communication and how we express ourselves and understand others. Blue stimulates the throat and aids the body's ability to heal and clear areas of elimination such as the lymphatic system and i.e.; blood, urine, water.

Indigo	This color helps in mental strength and assists the mind in gaining focus, clarity intuition and perception. Channel this color to connect a person with their higher guidance and to access their inner wisdom.
Violet	Violet connects us to all things, Oneness, the Divine and expands our consciousness.
Lavender	Lavender is used primarily in the higher chakras for calming and to relieve stress and anxiety in the mind and mental subtle body.
Silver	Silver stimulates the endocrine system and is the color we use with other colors when the body's energy is very depleted. It is also a good color to use to help the other colors integrate into the physical body.
Gold	Gold is the color of expansion and abundance. Channel gold into a person's brain to transmute negative energies and expand consciousness.
Diamond	This frequency of light works on a cellular and DNA level and is used at the third eye as well as the soul star.

Platinum	Platinum white light is the color or frequency that helps with the ascension process. Channel it into the soul star then bring it down into each chakra to fortify the system. Platinum works to expand the pineal gland.

Energetic Exercise: Grounding to Mother Earth

This exercise is for when we need to ground the physical body. Sometimes we can lose touch with the earth and may experience feelings of fearfulness and anxiety. To eradicate this fear, visualize pink or red roots growing from your root chakra, down through your legs and out the soles of your feet deep into the earth. Feel these roots spreading out into the soil and connecting with all the other roots from all the plants on the planet, the bushes, flowers, trees, grasslands and feel the energy from these roots as a warm, connective energy. Ask to be connected to the magnetic core of the Earth. Now feel the loving and supportive energy that Mother Earth is sending you, she is there providing you with everything you need, nourishing you and sustaining you. Breathe this warm pink nurturing energy up through the roots, into the soles of your feet, up through your legs and into the base / root chakra and see and feel the pink energy enveloping your entire being as if you are being cradled in the womb of the Earth. Feel that you are part of this earth, that you are connected, nourished and loved. Feel the support and love of your original Mother, Gaia, Mother earth.

Chapter Nine - Raising Your Vibration - The Basics - Returning to Your Natural State

"Everyone has a doctor in him or her; we just have to help it in its work. The natural healing force within each one of us is the greatest force in getting well."
~ Hippocrates

Along with changing my diet, meditating, yoga and exercise, I felt a strong urge to cleanse my body from parasites and clean my insides with liver and kidney cleanses. God was sending me clear messages on how to return my physical self to its natural state, hold the energy and allow myself to raise my vibration so that I could begin to merge with my Divine self within. We all need to return to our natural state of being, in order for our planet and our global community to heal and shift in a positive direction. It's time we grow up and take responsibility for our individual actions so that the human race may act as a healthy, cohesive force. I believe that this is what every single one of us on this planet needs to do at this time, become accountable for our actions.

If you've ever seen a flock of birds move, each bird is moving individually, and they all move together as one entity. It's a beautiful sight to see such harmony. Schools of fish and pods of dolphins work together too, instinctively. When you watch indigenous people dance together in ceremony, the entire community moves as one to the sound of the drum beat. I believe all human beings can become connected in this way, by returning to our natural states. If we as individuals can cultivate and maintain a healthy vibration and connect with our brothers and sisters who are also vibrating at the same frequency, then the possibility of creating a harmonious society increases.

True happiness is a result of how you use your consciousness. When you learn to use your consciousness a positive way, happiness is the natural consequence.

I look around me and see how many people are addicted to smoking and drinking and drugs, (both prescription and illegal). This state of addiction keeps an individual enslaved in a negative pattern so they never realize their potential; they do not experience overall happiness and cannot contribute to society. By existing at this lower vibration, they become a burden to themselves, their families and society in general. I know this well as I was once an addict.

This is a good example of why we need to raise our vibration. If you become aware of the energy that you emit, you can see what needs to be adjusted in your life to become a person who is whole, healthy and gives back to society. Look at your life and see if you are adding or subtracting from your world just by how you are living your life. Are you living your purpose, does your work feel meaningful and satisfying? Do you have healthy relationships? Do you have a healthy body? Are you experiencing higher emotions such as joy, compassion, love and happiness? Do you 'give back' or serve in some way to your community? Do you know and love yourself? Do you feel spiritually connected? Do you know our Great God?

Attaining a higher vibration brings you closer to source and brings you higher awareness, a higher consciousness and the power to create greater happiness in your life, which will also affect the greater population and all life on the planet.

We as a society are so out of balance and the only way to return to balance is by balancing ourselves, one by one, individually. Start with YOU. Lead and teach by example.

Human beings are very powerful, but most people do not believe that they are. You must not concern yourself with changing or fixing others, you must take care of yourself first. For example, when the flight attendants give directions about what to do if there is an in-flight emergency, when the oxygen mask drops down, you never give the oxygen mask to your child first, because you may pass out, and then you run the risk of both of you dying. You are instructed to put the oxygen mask on first to ensure that you remain conscious so then you can help the child or whoever is next to you. Well this is really no different; help yourself first before you attempt to help others.

We give our power away every day in so many ways; by working in jobs that we hate just to pay the rent, by feeding our addictions, by staying in relationships that are not healthy for us, by believing that we don't deserve the best in life.

We must reclaim our own power. The way to gain our power back is by making ourselves whole on every level. This starts with the physical body. You must give the body what it needs and stop hurting it in any way. You must nurture your body as you would a new born baby, with deep love, care and affection. The art of self care is generally not taught to us so it is up to us to learn how to treat our bodies with excellent care and attention.

Then you must emotionally give to yourself all the love you need. If you notice that you are criticizing yourself and beating yourself up, begin to change that inner dialogue to become loving and supportive. Treat yourself as you would a best friend. Would you berate and criticize your best friend? Chances are you wouldn't, so why treat yourself that way? Ways to love and nurture you are:

1. Eat high vibrational, whole foods and drink pure water
2. Exercise regularly & practice yoga
3. Get plenty of rest
4. Meditate & pray
5. Take necessary vitamins and supplements
6. Think positive and loving thoughts toward yourself and others

7. Surround yourself with loving, high vibrational, supportive people

8. Engage in meaningful work that satisfies you

9. Learn to give freely

10. Grow your connection with Spirit

11. Incorporate crystals and essential oils into your daily life

12. Work with the energy, the love light

13. Don't place yourself in situations that are harmful or do things you may later regret

14. Give yourself credit for the steps you have taken toward wellness so far

You must nurture your physical body into alignment. I've had clients come in who are depressed and anxious and the first thing I ask them is what is their diet and lifestyle? What are they putting into their body every day? If you are consuming a pot of coffee a day, and a bottle of wine every night, chances are, there will be a physical imbalance that will affect you on all the other levels. Do not expect to feel physically, mentally, emotionally & spiritually balanced if your organs are out of balance.

Your kidneys, liver, spleen, stomach, small and large intestines, lungs, pancreas, heart, brain, gallbladder and bladder are designed to work harmoniously for perfect health. Just like a healthy ecosystem in the natural world; the lakes, rivers, grasslands, soil, bogs, shrubs, trees, flowers, animals, insects and birds all interact beautifully with one another to create a perfect ecological environment that supports and sustains itself for optimum health and growth.

What happens when toxic pollutants are emptied into a lake? Over time the pollutant will affect the entire environment and throw it out of balance. Everything else around it will adjust to the pollutant in order to counteract the negative effect. If the toxic waste continues to be dumped into the lake, you will see a very negative influence on all parts of the ecological system. This example is a metaphor for our bodies. If you continue to poison your body with pollutants, something will eventually break down and the entire human being will be compromised. Everything is connected and we must honor this truth. The age-old saying of everything in moderation is so trite, but so true.

A person who drinks heavily and smokes is inflicting severe damage to their body. This type of physical abuse affects every organ, the mind and the emotions of the human being. Any of the negative emotions stemming from fear such as anger, resentment, hatred, depression and helplessness carried within our cells creates a difficult and miserable existence. This state of being is simply unhealthy.

Everything we ingest in our body affects us at a cellular level, within every organ, every system, it's all interconnected. Let's take a look at some of the organs.

The Organs - Each organ has an emotion attached to it. If you have anger issues, look to your liver. If we look at the teachings of Chinese Medicine, it is easy to see how every organ contributes to maintaining good health. Here are a few examples:

Heart

Heart Function - Regulates the heart and blood vessels. Responsible for even and regular pulse. Influences vitality and spirit. Connected with the tongue, complexion, and arteries.

125

Emotions when imbalanced- lack of enthusiasm and vitality, mental restlessness, depression, insomnia and despair.

Symptoms of Heart Imbalance - Insomnia, heart palpitations and irregular heartbeat, excessive dreaming, poor long-term memory, psychological disorders.

Kidney

Kidney Function - Key organ for sustaining life. Controls our will power and provides us with the motivation to do things in life. Responsible for reproduction, growth and development, and maturation. Involved with lungs in water metabolism and respiration. Connected with bones, teeth, ears, and head hair.

Emotions when imbalanced - fear, weak will power, insecure, aloof and isolated.

Symptoms of Kidney Imbalance - Frequent urination, urinary incontinence, night sweats, dry mouth, poor short-term memory, low back pain, ringing in the ears, hearing loss, and other ear conditions. Premature grey hair, hair loss, and osteoporosis.

Liver

Liver Function - Involved in the smooth flow of energy and blood throughout the body. Regulates bile secretion, stores blood, and is connected with the tendons, nails, and eyes.

Emotions when imbalanced - anger, resentment, frustration, irritability, bitterness, "flying off the handle".

Symptoms of Liver Imbalance - breast distension, menstrual pain, headache, irritability, inappropriate anger, dizziness, dry, red eyes and other eye conditions, tendonitis.

Lung

Lung Function - Respiration. Forms energy from air, and helps to distribute it throughout the body. Works with the kidney to regulate water metabolism. Important in the immune system and resistance to viruses and bacteria. Regulates sweat glands and body hair, and provides moisture to the skin.

Emotions when imbalanced - grief, sadness, detachment.

Symptoms of Lung Imbalance - Shortness of breath and shallow breathing, sweating, fatigue, cough, frequent cold and flu, allergies, asthma, and other lung conditions. Dry skin. Depression and crying.

Spleen

Spleen Function - Food digestion and nutrient absorption. Helps in the formation of blood and energy. Keeps blood in the blood vessels. Connected with muscles, mouth, and lips. Involved in thinking, studying, and memory.

Emotions when imbalanced - worry, dwelling or focusing too much on a particular topic, excessive mental work.

Symptoms of Spleen Imbalance - Tired, loss of appetite, mucus discharge, poor digestion, abdominal distension, loose stools or diarrhea. Weak muscles, pale lips. Bruising, excess menstrual blood flow, and other bleeding disorders.

We can balance the organs by the foods we put into our body. It takes discipline to choose healthy food, but once you learn how to make the right choices, you will be rewarded with good health. It's that simple. If you want to treat yourself to alcoholic beverages, sugar filled desserts and cakes, I don't recommend it but if you must do it with moderation so that the body doesn't start to crave these items over what it really needs to feel good. If you need a stimulant every morning to get you going and a depressant every night to wind you down, then you are creating an imbalance in your body.

You've heard the saying, "You are what you eat." It's so true. Raw diets are very popular these days. Raw foods can be handled by some people, they are harder to digest than cooked foods. I cannot eat a raw food diet because of my alcoholic past. Whenever I have tried to eat mostly raw foods, my blood sugar levels are affected and my energy wanes dramatically. I need to eat cooked foods that consist mostly of vegetables like squashes, sweet potatoes, legumes and greens as warm, nurturing food is best for my system. I discovered this through Ayurveda, the Science of Life. Raw food is also not good for many people in their senior years because it is harder on the digestive system. Find out what works best for you by experimenting for yourself and consulting with a nutritionist or Ayurvedic practitioner.

Liver and gallbladder flushes are also an excellent way to bring the body back into balance over time. I also believe strongly in parasite cleanses and colonics. I do recommend that you consult a holistic practitioner or nutritionist before you begin any cleanse. You may need some preparation time so you don't shock the body.

Honor the body you are in, it is your soul's only home in this lifetime, its temple. Love your body. Cherish your body. Nurture your body. Listen to your body. Your body is very wise and knows exactly what it needs to be happy. If there is a part of your body that is in pain, talk to it. Close your eyes and take your awareness to your stomach. Ask it why it hurts. Then wait for the answer. Send it love and tell it you will take care of it. See what the response feels like. Develop a close relationship with your body, befriend it. It will reward you with good health, a firm foundation for leading a happy, productive life.

<u>Energetic Exercise</u>: Releasing Other People's "Stuff"

We tend to carry other people's stuff with us, though we often don't realize it. This can result in tense shoulders and a tight neck, not to mention headaches or a knot in our belly. There is a great exercise I recommend doing right before you go to sleep. Lie down, close your eyes, greet your Higher Self and ask him/her to place a column of white light next to your head. Now mentally go through and think of all the things that belong to other people you are carrying with you i.e.; (your husband's job issues, your child's problems at school, your mother's ill health, your friend's divorce) and just see all of those worries going into the white light, transferring from you into the white energy to be sent out to the Universe, cleansed, rebalanced and used for healing for (whatever you dedicate it for). Do this exercise nightly for as long as you need to. After you finish, reaffirm silently to yourself that you love these people, but you don't need to carry their burdens. In fact, it will benefit them more if you are lighter and healthier by not carrying their stuff for them. Then wash white light over you and see yourself totally free of other's problems. Thank your Higher Self and go to sleep worry free!

Chapter Ten - Connection with your Higher Self

"Bring into play the almighty power within you, so that on the stage of life you can fulfill your high destined role."
~Paramahansa Yogananda

Our Higher Self is the most spiritual and perfect part of each of us, which exists on another (non-physical) dimension. The Higher Self is the energy of our true-self, the divine within us, our cosmic consciousness. It is beyond our body, mind, personality and our feelings; it is our pure essence, our Spirit. The Higher Self is our presence of being, our God-self.

When our soul incarnates into our physical body in this lifetime, all of our Divine Self energy cannot come into the human form. Our Divine Self or Higher Self carries a high frequency that is not compatible with the lower vibrations of the Earth plane. If all of the Divine or soul energy were to come into the human body, it would not be able to withstand the high frequencies so only a spark of our Divine Self comes into the body, the rest, our Higher Self, remains on another level of the astral plane, another dimension, where it vibrates at a higher frequency. We access that level of ourselves through meditation, through connection on the etheric level through energy, or light. The Higher Self is connected to us through an energetic tube, which connects to the top of the head.

The purpose of our Higher Self is to work with us by keeping us on our path so that we may complete our life's purpose and learn the lessons we agreed to before we incarnated into this body in this lifetime. The Higher Self will eventually bring us back to God if we stay on our path and allow it to help us.

All of our physical, mental, emotional, and spiritual issues we experience in this life are designed to help us meet our life's purpose. If we tune into and listen to our Higher Self, it can help us make the best choices as we navigate through our lives. Our Higher Self has been with our soul in every lifetime and can see what is behind us, our past, what is before us, our future and therefore really is the most qualified being for guiding us.

The idea is that we create our existence with our Higher Self and God in every thought we think and in every choice we make. That is why we are called co-creators. Become aware of your thoughts and ensure they are positive because they create your reality.

The founder of the Australian Association of Applied Parapsychology, Rhonnda Elizabeth Stewart states, "The Higher Self is another part of your consciousness, a higher part of you. By re-linking with that part of ourselves that lives in a higher level of awareness and has a greater level of understanding, it can help us with our growth and development. The Higher Self is our ultimate teacher and once you connect with your Higher Self you have opened the door to your unlimited potential. As you communicate with your Higher Self, you will receive answers and expand your understanding and awareness that can affect all areas of your life so you can create and manifest whatever you choose. It is important to remember that if you are thinking, you are not communicating with your Higher Self or guidance, you are working with your own thoughts, your own unconscious thinking. If there is a sense, a feeling or a "knowingness", then you are communicating with your Higher Self."

To know your Higher Self is one of the most important connections you will make in your lifetime. Converse with your

Higher Self daily, acknowledging their existence and you will begin to re-connect to a source of infinite wisdom and love.

I continuously ask my Higher Self questions pertaining to what is happening in my life. I find that I receive answers, in one form or another such as a thought or idea popping into my head, through a book, a magazine article, a TV show, or a conversation with a friend. Sometimes it may take a while to get the answer and I would have forgotten the question!

Growth was a little slow for me in the beginning. I found when I first started working with my Higher Self, that the answer usually came within a week of asking or sooner. The trick is to remember what you asked and then watch or listen for the answer and be willing to accept the answer once you receive it , learn to trust the information you are being given. This is how you receive guidance. Growing this relationship will grow your intuition and give you greater trust in yourself and your decisions and choices.

I am now at the point where I don't really ask too many questions of my Higher Self, I find that I am supported in manifesting what I need. I have surrendered my will to the Divine's will and so my desires are aligned with my highest good and the highest good of all, living a life in service. There is a strong link now between us so that it feels that I am living as my Higher Self more and more each day. I believe this is part of the Ascension process, or my path back to God. I still have my personality which is my individual imprint of who I am as a human being and within my personality I still have wounds which I continue to work on. I also still make mistakes, this hasn't changed as I will always have lessons to learn. What has changed is the recovery process after the mistake has been made. There seems to be an ability to shift more quickly and learn the lesson gracefully.

Being spiritual doesn't mean that we lose our personality, our sense of humor, or our individuality, with our own expression of who we are, as long we are in our body (embodied), we will maintain a personality, it is part of being human. Even as I become more and more spiritual carrying a higher frequency and aligning with my God-Self, I will still love Reggae music, enjoy dressing in my own comfortable style with cowboy boots, scarves and crystal jewelry, dancing like a wild bohemian gypsy under the moon, hiking in the mountains with my dog, eating Indian food and all those things that make up my personality in this lifetime. We do not lose our human self as we become more spiritual. The idea is that we move away from the ego-mind that limits us and remember our Divine nature as the spiritual light beings that we are encased within a human form.

When I began to work with my Higher Self and raise my vibration, the process was turbulent. Looking back I can see that my spiritual progress was similar to a set of stairs. As I incorporated spiritual truths or understandings into my awareness, my vibration would rise, just like taking a step up. Then I hit a plateau where I was processing the information into my physical being so that I had a true understanding of it in my entire being, on every level. Quite often while processing the information, a feeling of discomfort or awkwardness permeated my life just like when a child experiences growing pains. The discomfort came from laying down the ego and slowly replacing it with the wisdom of the Divine. The ego does not want to leave, so as it feels threatened, it lashes out like a spoiled child. It often felt like I was going backwards in my development as the ego struggled fiercely to stay in power and negative thinking would infiltrate my mind and create doubt.

Over the past eleven years of working with my Higher Self and raising my vibration, this cycle has continued with a jump upward and then a time of processing or feeling in the void, thereby creating a pattern of up and across, up and across, or "steps".

This is also a time when old likes or preferences are let go of and replaced with new likes. It is essentially the beginning of the ego fading away, which can feel very uncomfortable, as the western society caters to the ego. All media is geared toward getting us to buy something in order for us to feel good about ourselves. Our Western society is structured around commercialism and money.

We often hold onto old beliefs because we attach emotional feelings to it and the feeling becomes very strongly embedded in our being. Changing one's mentality and behavior can be painful. When we don't get what we want, we feel we are being deprived of that which makes us happy. Once we let go of what we think will make us happy and let God give us what we need to evolve, we can understand that we are being taught to accept that which is for our highest good and for the good of all.

A very basic analogy of this is a child wanting a lollipop and when the mother takes it away, the child cries. The mother knows the lollipop is not good for the child and by not giving them the lollipop, they are looking out for the child although the child certainly doesn't see it this way. When our changing beliefs and behavior affect others in our lives that are used to us thinking and acting a certain way, these friends and family may be confused by our new conduct and feel threatened. They may want the "old" us to return so the feeling is familiar and safe. The repercussions of our changes can be far-reaching.

God is within each of us, we are made in the image of God. It took me nearly two years of meditating at least three to five times a week for an hour or longer to break through or re-connect with my Higher Self. That was from 2001 - 2003, but the vibrations of the Earth are constantly speeding up so even since that time it has become easier for people to transcend the veil and to connect with their Higher Selves.

When my Higher Self first came through, I saw a face in my meditation, the only way I can describe it is that it was like a face coming through an energetic force field or a violet blanket and when it came through the other side, where it took on form, in a beautiful violet energy, it winked and smiled at me! That week I saw two different photographs of a similar image at two different times in my daily routine, once in a book of photography an artist had shot a face framed out of shadow and light with the subject winking and another photograph was in a magazine of a boy in India lying in water and only his face was protruding and it was confirmation for me that I had seen what I had seen, it was as if my Higher Self was saying, "Yes, your vision of me is real, I am real, I exist".

Everything changed once I re-connected with my Higher Self, I definitely had an epiphany, I felt all the power of God within me then and I knew my potential was unlimited. I am a human being, but a divine and beautiful spiritual being in human form just as God had intended. To not have known this truth before was why I suffered so much, because I was only living a fraction of who I truly am. I thought I was all alone in this world and the burden seemed so heavy. I thought I had to navigate this world alone and the task at hand seemed impossible.

The ego is a powerful force and I still get caught in the illusion that I am my mind or body or emotions, I still suffer at times. I have to remind myself every single day of the truth; I believe that is the purpose of a daily spiritual practice, to keep oneself aligned with this truth. One good habit to practice is to wake up and thank the Creator for this life, for the beautiful planet and all life forms, and for our family, friends, lessons and blessings. Lessons really are blessings in the end, so I like to call them "blessons". To only see ourselves as human and not divine is a limiting false illusion. Whenever I find myself suffering on a particular day, I remind myself where I came from and where I am today. Spiritual growth in my life has been enormous and where I am now is a much better place than where I used to be. My consciousness has evolved and as it continues to evolve, it feels wonderful, light and free.

The way to re-connect with our Higher Self is through intention and meditation. Meditate, meditate, meditate. We must open up a dialogue, just like we would with a new friend, and allow time and space for a response. I truly believe that this is the most important relationship you'll ever have in your lifetime. It is the relationship with your true self. Once you make this connection

141

you must know that your Higher Self will never abandon you, will always love you unconditionally, guide you to your best choice, support you in times of despair and generally be your best friend. You can choose to do Vibrational healing without your Higher Self, but the question begs, why would you? Put the master in charge and you will get the best results.

When you first begin to re-connect with your Higher Self, meditate 20 minutes every day and ask your Higher Self to join you. Take your awareness to a sphere of energy above your head. Attune to this energy and know this energy to be your Higher Self. Spend time breathing deeply, relaxing your body, letting all thoughts fall away and connecting to the energy of your Higher Self in the realm of "nothingness". As you become familiar with this energy, you can begin to ask questions in your meditation. The key to reconnection is being consistent and spending time with the intention to connect.

Energetic Exercise: Protective Bubble

The world is full of negative and positive energy and it is wise to protect ourselves from the negative. Just as you would wear a raincoat in the rain, it is advantageous to protect your energetic field from all the negative energy you encounter in your day. For self-protection, open up with white light, say hello to your Higher Self and then visualize a column of blue energy coming down from the Universe and surround your entire body with a blue bubble - confirm with your Higher Self that this blue bubble is for protection. This blue capsule acts energetically as a filter, to keep good energy in and release any of your own negative energy to the Universe to be cleansed without letting anyone else's negative energy infiltrate your energetic field. If there are particular individuals you are dealing with regularly that are giving off a lot of negativity, ask your Higher Self to put mirrors around you so that the negative energy they send out bounces off of you and back at them with love - always with love. For extra protection, call upon Archangel Michael and ask him to protect your energy from other's negativity. He is a multi-dimensional being and can be in many different places at once. Also ask when you go to sleep to be protected while your astral body travels and to only travel to the highest levels of the astral.

Chapter Eleven - The Chakra System

"People are like stained-glass windows. They sparkle and shine when the sun is out, but when the darkness sets in their true beauty is revealed only if there is light from within."
~Elisabeth Kübler-Ross

Chakra means "wheel" in Sanskrit. The body has spinning energy centers that look like spinning wheels and are called, chakras, pronounced chuk rah. The physical body contains hundreds of these energy centers that are the key to the operation of our being. Through these energy centers we receive, transmit and process life's energies. Ideally, we want to clear them of the blocks, the old painful issues, and negative beliefs and fill them with positivity on all levels including our thoughts and intentions.

We have seven main chakra centers and each main center is connected to different aspects of ourselves as spiritual beings in a physical form. These aspects, the physical, emotional, mental and spiritual all combine to make up the whole. On the physical level each chakra governs an endocrine gland and organ that are all interconnected and with every system in the body which resonate the same frequency. Our emotions and thoughts have a great impact on what we experience in our life, therefore we need to change our negative thinking into positive thinking, to align with our Highest self.

The chakras, or energy centers, function as valves, regulating the flow of energy through our energy system. These "vortex's" draw in information from our surroundings. So much of what is going on around us is happening on an energetic, subconscious level and is not apparent to the human eye. This information can be anything from a color vibration to ultra-violet ray to a radio or micro wave, or coded information to another person's aura. In essence, our chakras receive the health of our environment, including the people we are in contact with (that's why other people's moods have an effect on us).

Every organ, gland and body system is connected to a chakra and each chakra is connected to a color frequency. For example, the heart chakra governs the thymus gland and it is also in charge of the functioning of the heart, lungs, bronchial system, lymph glands, secondary circulatory system, immune system as well as the arm and hands. The heart chakra resonates to the color green. The seven main chakra centers are aligned along the spinal column. If there are disturbances on any level, this shows in the chakra's vitality level. Also each of the seven main chakras is their own intelligence center. This means that each chakra is not only associated with our physical health but also governs aspects connected to our emotional, mental and spiritual selves. To help balance a chakra-whether on an emotional, intellectual, physical or spiritual level-we need to bring in the chakra (color) vibration, which resonates at the same frequency.

The benefit of learning about your own chakra system is for you to understand on a whole (whole = body, mind and spirit in harmony) that when all elements of you (all of your seven chakra centers) are communicating equally and working in alliance with each other, you will have little or no energy disorders. For example, if the mental part of you is powerful and so are the physical, emotional and spiritual parts of you equally as strong, it is then that you feel at your optimum level.

The chakras are the energetic highways that link our physical bodies to our subtle bodies and all the dimensions beyond where the unseen information travels every second. It's important that we have an understanding of their basic function, because when issues surface in our lives, we can locate them on our energetic map, our chakra system, it then becomes easier to work on the issue if we know where it resides.

The human energy system is devised of the chakras and the subtle bodies that are layered around our physical body. The subtle bodies start with the etheric body which is the medium for vital life force energy, the emotional body, which governs the desires and emotions, the mental body, which is the medium for the lower mind, and the causal, or seed body, which governs the higher mind and the blue print for our life. Each of these subtle bodies needs to be cleared of debris to become fully realized. Vibrational healing will help to remove the unwanted blocks within the subtle bodies.

Nowadays, we live in a chaotic world and often forget about our "whole." We put too much emphasis on independence and very little on interdependence. Our chakras are interdependent on each other for harmony and balance.

By channeling light into the chakras, we are affecting the electromagnetic energy which creates a chemical reaction through the endocrine system which then creates change in the physical body. The endocrine system produces natural chemicals or hormones such as adrenaline, insulin, estrogen and progesterone which are secreted into the bloodstream from corresponding organs to stimulate or inhibit certain physical processes. The mind and thoughts affect the endocrine system, and our thoughts and beliefs will affect our bodies. That is why the beliefs and thoughts must change to support the energetic work that a practitioner provides. The practitioner is there to assist with the transformation through counseling and to support it with the source energy by realigning the energy field. It is up to the individual to uncover the truth within and discard the old misaligned beliefs that no longer serve them. If a person holds onto beliefs that have not worked for them, they can't expect those same beliefs to suddenly work now. There's the saying, "If you do what you did, you get what you got.", so the element of changing or letting go of one's beliefs is important to one's evolution.

There are 7 major chakras in the body as well as the Earth Star and the Transpersonal Point or Soul Star.

Earth Star

Below the feet is the Earth Star or Grounding Chakra, which represents our connection with the earth plane. This chakra anchors us to the planet and connects us to the earth's electromagnetic field. Traumatic events can knock your earth star off center and make you feel ungrounded. It also represents the path you are on in this lifetime. If you are undecided about which way to go and are going through tremendous change in your life, your earth star can be affected. A depleted earth star chakra is common with people who travel a lot. People whose awareness rests mostly in their higher chakras tend to become ungrounded and need to constantly run energy through their earth star to anchor them to the physical, earth plane. The best way to do this is from the root chakra, down through the feet chakras and into the earth star below.

Base Chakra

In Sanskrit, *Muladhara*, meaning root or support. It is located between the genitals and the anus and its endocrine gland is the adrenals. It is associated with the color red, the element earth and the physical sense of smell. The root chakra is connected to the Mother and the family unit, so any issues you have with your family will manifest as imbalances here. This chakra provides grounding and support for the entire energy system and is about security and survival. It is the foundation for materializing our ideas and intentions. Its function supports healthy blood, bones and nerves. When blocked, the base chakra brings about fear of survival and blocks our ability to manifest and creates the feeling of being a victim who blames others, feeling needy and ungrounded. When this chakra is balanced we feel connected to Mother Earth and feel she provides for all the physical and emotional security we need to feel nourished, supported and nurtured.

Sacral Chakra

Svadhishthana, or sweetness. It is associated with the color orange, the element water and the physical sense of taste and appetite. The sacral chakra located below the belly button and the ovaries and testes are the endocrine gland. The second chakra is about our desires, our creativity, sexuality and sensuality. This is also where we hold onto old belief systems.

With a clear second chakra, we embrace change and attract more of what we really want, we also give birth to new creative energy in the form of ideas. Governed by the element of water, it's important this chakra be flowing as our emotions need to be flowing through us so we don't get stuck. If the second chakra is blocked we may feel guilty, untrusting or fearful of change. With a healthy second chakra we are able to feel and express joy, own our sexuality and feel our emotions in balance and supporting our passionate creative desires.

The Solar Plexus Chakra

Manipura, or lustrous gem. It is yellow, the element is fire and its relationship to the sun and it is associated with the physical sense of sight. This chakra is at our solar plexus and the pancreas is the endocrine gland. The third chakra is about self empowerment, our will and supports self belief and integrity. It's where we hold our sense of self and use our personal power to carry out our intentions. Governed by the fire element, the third chakra is where we take action. When blocked, we don't have enough fire, or will to take action. We can become passive and unable to muster up the discipline, courage or confidence required to create what we want and reach our full potential. A vibrant and balanced solar plexus chakra helps us manifest a life that expresses all of who we are including our attitude, values, visions and goals.

The Heart Chakra

Anahata, or unstruck. It is associated with two colors - emerald green and rose pink, with the element air, and with the physical sense of touch. It is located at the heart center and the endocrine gland is the thymus. This chakra is about compassion, self love and the ability to forgive and love unconditionally. It is where we connect in union with others in all relationships including marriage. When the heart chakra is blocked we feel sad; when it's clear we feel joy. A closed heart chakra can keep us from connecting with others or from moving on from past hurts. When we release grief and loss through forgiveness and love, we attract to us the love we want in our lives. A healthy heart chakra is apparent in one who has mastered the ability to love oneself and others unconditionally.

Throat Chakra

Vishuddhi, or purification. It is light blue, and the element is ether. This chakra is located at the throat and the thyroid is the endocrine gland. When our throat chakra is clear, we easily speak our truth by connecting and communicating with others from our heart through our voice. This chakra is about our choices, expressing our needs, intentions and creativity. The throat chakra expresses our creative identity and is an important part of creating and acting on our intentions. A balanced throat chakra is apparent when we are able to express our needs lovingly and powerfully and make choices that support our ability to fulfill our potential in this lifetime.

Third Eye

Ajna, meaning to perceive, to know. It is indigo and the element is vibration - the inner sound. The third eye is located between the eyebrows and the pineal gland is its corresponding endocrine gland. It is where we receive inspiration and intuition, and where we connect with our Higher Self through clairvoyance, the ability to see beyond the illusion. We also want to achieve a balanced intellect and intuition with the left brain and right brain synchronized. A blocked third eye inhibits our imagination and ability to see alternatives and keeps us trapped in our old patterns of thinking. We could be drawn to fantasies, illusions or obsessions rather than intuition and inspiration. With a clear third eye we will be open to a flow of new ideas and inspiration, creative energy and the wisdom and guidance that is available to us from our true self.

Crown Chakra

Sahasrara, or thousand-fold. It is represented by a violet lotus with a thousand petals of white light. Its element is spiritual vibration, inner light and it's associated with beyond self and the connection to all things. The crown chakra, located at the top of the head, is where our Divine self connects to the human body and where we experience oneness with the universe. The endocrine gland associated with the crown chakra is the pituitary gland. This is where we receive divine wisdom and the flow of higher consciousness. This chakra supports our entire being by bringing in clear, cosmic energy. A blocked crown chakra could keep us aligned with old, outdated beliefs that no longer serve us or create confusion, closed-mindedness and a feeling that we are separate. With a balanced crown chakra we are able to continue to evolve and connect to our true essence, readily

154

letting go of old beliefs and aligning ourselves with the truth of who we are, bringing us ever closer to God, the Creator.

The Transpersonal point is located above the head and connects us with other dimensions. This is where Spirit enters into our body at birth and leaves at death the point where we are connected to Source. It holds the energies of past lives and contains the information of why we incarnated into this life, or our master blue print. The color is platinum.

The chakras connect and affect the 72,000 nadis, or energy channels that parallel the network of nerves throughout the body which carries the flow of the subtle energy system. The three most important nadis are the Sushumna, Ida and Pingala. Ida is the left channel, it is feminine, the moon, cool air and is the channel that runs from the base chakra to the left nostril. Pingala is the right channel, it is masculine, the sun and is warm air and runs from the base chakra to the right nostril. Sushumna is the central channel running along the spine from the base chakra to the crown chakra and is connected to all chakras through stems. The sushumna brings in the vital life force energy or prana into and out of our energy system through our crown and base chakras.

Everything that comprises the human and spiritual being is interrelated amongst a vast, complex and beautiful network, a grand design created by God. The energetic affects the physical, which affects the emotional which affects the mental, it is truly amazing. Vibrational healing helps to align all of these different aspects of the self, to raise one's vibration to move ever toward well-being and embodying the Divine self.

<u>Energetic Exercise:</u> Pink Bubble of Manifestation

In a meditative state, visualize yourself exactly as you want to be, happy, healthy and smiling. See as many details as you possibly can, notice what you are wearing, who you are with, what you are doing. See and feel the joy that you hold inside that shines brightly from your heart center and from your eyes. Now put a pink bubble around this vision of yourself and send it out into the Universe and ask that it be made a reality. You can do this exercise for yourself or any of your loved ones at any time.

Chapter Twelve - Clearing, Rebalancing and Protecting Your Energy Field

"What is meditation? Becoming one with the soul. It means banishing the consciousness of being related to the body and to human limitations, and trying to remember that one is a soul."
~Paramahansa Yogananda

It is imperative that we learn how to cleanse, rebalance and protect our own energy field. We are surrounded by energy, both positive and negative and we want to keep the negative or inferior force from entering our field. Negative forces can come from other people and entities who feed off of fear. To raise our vibration and align ourselves with our divinity, we must keep a clear, balanced energy field. We cleanse, rebalance and protect ourselves by connecting with our Higher Self in meditation.

Meditation

- Benefits of Meditation
- Greater creativity and insight
- Improves clarity of the mind and intuition
- Increases feelings of vitality and rejuvenation

158

- Increases emotional stability
- Leads to a deeper level of relaxation by reducing tension

There are many different ways to meditate - but all share similar basic guidelines. The body position is important; when you are in a seated position, you are aligned with the spiritual plane as opposed to a horizontal position, which is aligned with the physical plane. That is why it is recommended that you meditate sitting up with the spine straight so that the divine energy comes down through the top of the head or crown chakra. Place your hands on your thighs facing up to receive the energy or cross your palms in your lap. Your feet are on the floor allowing the energy to run out through them and into the earth, or you are seated on the floor, with your legs folded.

Your breathing is slow and steady - you can practice breathing in through your nose 6 counts, and out through your nose 8 counts. Bring the breath all the way down into your abdomen first, and then fill the lungs. Take 6 counts in, hold it 1 count and breathe out 8 counts. You can play with the number of counts you hold it such as 8 in 10 out or 10 in 12 out. As a beginner, you may wish to do 6 counts in and 8 counts out, after a while it will become easier to take longer breaths.

Your deep breathing will relax the body. Scan the body from head to toe, concentrate on releasing the tension from each part. Bring your attention to your forehead, temples, skull, eyes, ears, jaw, tongue, neck, throat, shoulders, heart, chest, arms, lungs, stomach, pelvic floor, hips, butt, thighs, knees, calves, ankles and feet. Now that you have scanned your body, move back through it to make sure you have released all tension. The mind should be alert, the body relaxed. The goal is to let go of all thoughts and transcend the so mind so you can listen to Spirit. If thoughts arise, simply let them go and continue to bring your focus back to a state of emptiness. In this state is where we connect to the divine within, or source. The infinite space, the oneness, we are connected to all things, God is in us. The feeling you are seeking is total bliss - completely relaxed yet mentally alert and a feeling of connectedness and mild, buzzy ecstasy.

While meditating it's important to focus your closed eyes at the point between your eyebrows, which is your third eye. This pulls the energy in the brain forward to the frontal lobes, located in the neocortex, the most evolutionarily advanced portion of the brain and away from the Limbic system, otherwise known as "the emotional brain", a primitive portion of the brain. The Limbic system is deep in the center of the brain and is among other things, associated with survival instincts including fight or flight and primitive emotions such as fear, rage and aggression. People with over-active limbic systems show phobias, anxieties and poor anger management. When the energy is taken away from the limbic brain, we see a decrease in depression, anger, anxiety, insomnia and an improved mood control.

With meditation and focusing on the third eye, we also see an increased number and functionality of cells in the frontal lobe resulting in calmer, non reactive behavior, and heightened states of attention, ability to gain deep insights and overcome negative patterns. This also allows both hemispheres of the brain to relate better, or "brain synchronicity" which results in clear, creative thinking and better intuition. Meditation decreases oxygen consumption, heart rate and respiratory rate, helping lower stress levels.

Aim for 5 - 20 minutes a day. It may seem difficult at first, but just like anything, it takes practice. If at first you feel you are not achieving the desired results, do not give up! Work your way up to an hour a day. Meditation is a lifelong practice - so enjoy the journey!

Chakra Rebalance Meditation using Affirmations

The following chakra rebalance exercise brings light into your chakras raising your vibration. I have been doing it for eleven years and it has helped me to expand my light field and supports my evolution and transformation. It's so important to use the light to rebalance your energetic field on a regular and consistent basis. Once skilled at this form of rebalancing, you will start to feel your chakras realigning. Focus on the color coming into the chakra center, if you can't visualize the color, simply imagine the color in your mind and know that you are receiving this light. If you invoke the light, it must come to you, it is a Universal law.

The great thing is you can do it anywhere. I love to do it when sitting on a bus, or waiting in line somewhere, it's a wonderful way to pass the time. It isn't necessary to use the affirmations every time, simply bring in the light. The first step is to open up your energy field with white light and greet your Higher Self with love.

After opening up with the white light energy, which cleanses all negativity from your aura, bring in a red energy from the earth, up through your feet chakras and into your base chakra. Feel it and see the red energy swirling all around the base chakra asking it to rebalance and revitalize that chakra. Focus on the red energy, feel the chakra pulsing and expanding. Do this for anywhere from 3-5 minutes. Once you feel the red chakra shift, affirm that it is balanced. Root affirmation - my body is becoming more important to me, I nurture it constantly. I am connected to mother Earth and know the security of being grounded in the moment.

Next bring up an orange light through your feet chakras and into the sacral chakra, just below your belly button. Again, feel the orange energy enveloping the entire area and ask for the sacral chakra to be rejuvenated. Feel the energy out of the front of the body as well as the back. Sacral affirmation - Who I am is good enough. I am moving toward a time when I am totally happy and fulfilled. Life offers me everything I need for that journey. Pause, breathe. Affirm that the sacral chakra is balanced.

Now bring in a bright yellow light like the sun up from the earth and through the feet chakras into the solar plexus chakra and feel and see that yellow energy completely regenerating your yellow center. Solar plexus affirmation - I treat myself with honor and respect. I deserve all the love, respect, joy and prosperity that comes to me. I am open to receiving all of life's goodness. Affirm that solar plexus is balanced.

Beginning with the heart chakra you want to bring the light in from above you, from the divine. Make sure with each chakra, that you feel the energy out of the front of the chakra as well as the back. Spend time on each chakra, until you feel a shift and don't rush the process.

Moving up to the heart center, from above you, bring an emerald green into the heart, you may wish to intertwine this with a rose pink, so that there is a twirling double energy rebalancing your heart center. Remember to stay with the energy until you feel the expansion take place and affirm it is rebalanced. Heart affirmation - All past hurts I release into the hands of love. Love will set me free. I love myself for who I am and the potential within me. Affirm that the heart chakra is balanced.

Now bring down a beautiful sky blue energy into the throat chakra and feel it swirling all around, totally transforming every molecule of the blue chakra. Throat affirmation - What I have to say is worthy of being listened to. I delight in my self-expression and all my creative pursuits. Affirm that the throat chakra is balanced.

With strong intention, call upon the indigo light to enter into your third eye chakra and know it is illuminating and balancing your brow center. Third eye affirmation - I am full of wisdom. I trust my inner self to guide and protect me. The answers to all my questions lie within me. Affirm that the third eye chakra is balanced.

Finally bring down the velvety violet light energy into the crown and all around your entire head and feel the oneness, the complete connection to all that is as you expand and realign this center with the Divine. Crown affirmation - I tune into the Union with my Higher Power. I choose to transform myself and become free. I am who I am and I glory in that. I AM THAT. Affirm that the crown chakra is balanced.

Now is a good time to take your focus back to your base and see and feel the red and work your way up through each chakra, attuning to each color, feeling that it is balanced and spinning in perfect harmony with the other chakras. If you feel that one chakra is weak, go back to that and focus on the light color that corresponds to it until you feel it strengthening.

This is such a wonderful exercise you can do for your light being every day. If at first you cannot feel the physical shifts within your body as you work on each chakra, be patient, the more you do it the more you will be sensitive to the energy.

Once your chakras are cleansed with the white light and rebalanced with the colors, invoke Archangel Michael and ask him to protect your energy field with a layer of blue energy, see it as a sheath that forms an egg shape around your body, then a layer of purple and finally a layer of gold energy. Then seal the entire energy field with three golden rings, like giant hula hoops

166

that come down from above around your aura into the earth. This protects your rebalanced field.

It is important to protect your energy when you are going out into the world, after you have finished working in the light. I do this when I leave my home or after I meditate or finish a Vibrational energy session. Rebalancing your chakras will increase and fortify your energy as you raise your vibration and align with your Higher Self. You must be the one who does the work to become self aware, shifting your negative patterns and evolving into a lighter, wiser, empowered and joyous being.

A special note for those people who are highly sensitive; make sure you protect your energy field at all times, this will help you to avoid overreacting to the harshness of loud noises, lights, negative energy and crowds.

I see a lot of people who have very open hearts who have been hurt because they are givers by nature, constantly giving to others and then being hurt when that loving, generous energy isn't returned in kind. They are often taken advantage of by others because they are so giving. It's important to learn to monitor your heart chakra, so that you do not give everything away and constantly feel betrayed or hurt. Imagine there is a window in your heart, for these people (the givers), the window is wide open. To avoid getting hurt over and over, put the fly screen down so you don't have to shut the window completely and close off your heart. This way the negative stuff stays out but there is still a flow of energy into and out of the heart. Learn to say no to protect your own self. People respect you when you say no. Give to those who will appreciate what you have to give.

Learning to manage our own energy field is so beneficial to our overall health and well-being. I wish we were all able to see energy and how it affects us, we can certainly feel it but because we can't see it, we tend to not think about it. Begin to think about your energy as a tangible force and take care of it by using these exercises I offer and by connecting with Archangel Michael and your Higher Self to help you to protect and rebalance your field every day.

Chapter Thirteen - How to Guide Energy

"The body is a self-healing organism, so it's really about clearing things out of the way so the body can heal itself."

~Barbara Brennan

The thing to remember about Vibrational healing is that you don't have to understand the science of it for healing to take place. A pilot is not required to know how to construct a plane and have complete knowledge of each part and how they work perfectly together allowing him to maneuver it through the air at 500 miles an hour, but nevertheless he is given lessons and instructions on how to fly the plane safely. In this chapter I am going to share with you how to direct the energy and the rest will be done through your intention, action and connection with your Higher Self and benevolent light beings. What you need to do is trust that what you are doing is working for the benefit of you or your client.

It is recommended that before you begin to channel energy as a light worker, you re-connect with your Higher Self through consistent meditations and intention. This may take anywhere from six months to two years, perhaps even sooner depending on the person and how much time they are investing. You will know when the reconnection has occurred. Ask for confirmation from your Higher Self that you have reconnected.

The first step in channeling energy is to open up by bringing white light down through your crown chakra and connecting to your Higher Self by acknowledging them. Next, with thought intention, wash your subject/client in white light to open them up. Washing both of you in white light instantly cleanses negativity and creates a space for the healing to take place. Also, the other point of doing this is to ensure that you are not taking on their stuff and they are not taking on your stuff. The energy will simply run through you without your stuff attaching to them. You must set this intention in your mind at the beginning of each session. Once you open up, your Higher Self is connecting with their Higher Self to open the lines of communication. It is recommended to do healing sessions alone without other people in the room apart from the healee.

Next step is to lay down a mat of green energy on the floor / ground, which collects any negative or residual energy that is released during the session. With the intention of doing so, channel green energy with your dominant hand, the same hand you write with, underneath the massage table and covering the entire floor of the room and then create a column of energy that extends from the base of the massage table in a column that extends up into the Universe. As you are doing this say silently, "I now create a mat of green energy to collect any residual or negative energy to be sent out through this column into the Universe to be cleansed and rebalanced and used for _____ then dedicate it to whatever you wish the healing energy be used for. I usually nominate a friend, relative or the client and will say something like, "…healing for my uncle's eyes, or, extra healing for Betty's knee." I also like to dedicate the healing energy for planetary healing or all beings in the cosmos. The planet can always use a little healing! Now the green energy mat is there and the column is taking away all the negative stuff, you're good to go.

Next, say a prayer of intention and gratitude. For example, I say, "Dear God, Goddess, Spirit, I ask that you make me a pure channel for your healing light to help i.e.; Mark -(say their name) where he is on his path at this time. I ask that this light work with him for his highest good and the good of all. (It's important to note that some people are meant to be sick to learn a particular lesson and their soul has agreed to be sick, so that is why you must say "for their highest good".) Please recede my ego. I connect to my Higher Self, my own Divinity and Divine Mother, and connect also to Mark's Higher Self and Divinity and ask that I am given any information that will help Mark. Please guide my thoughts, words and actions. I ask that only the Truth be spoken here today. I ask that any beings present that do not work in the light or are not aligned with God must leave immediately. I work with you now in total love, service and devotion. Aum."

Then check each chakra to see whether it is balanced, blocked, depleted or torn. Highly experienced energy therapists can check the energy of the chakra with their "feeling", or non-dominant hand, for me that is my left hand as I channel with my right hand. The hand you write with will generally be your channeling hand and your feeling hand will be the other hand.

One way to check the energy of a chakra is to use a pendulum as it is accurate and always tells you exactly what the energy is doing. First you must ascertain what balanced, blocked, depleted

172

and torn are for the pendulum by saying the word out loud and seeing what the pendulum does. This is how to establish a relationship with the pendulum. For example, when I say, "blocked", the pendulum spins counterclockwise, to the left, then the chakra is blocked, or if the pendulum swings back and forth, the chakra is depleted and if the pendulum doesn't spin at all the chakra is torn. If the pendulum spins clockwise, to the right, the chakra is balanced. Sometimes the pendulum will swing in a small circle to the right, which means the chakra just needs a boost of energy to get it vibrating to maximum potential. When the pendulum spins to the right in a diameter of between 6 to 10 inches, it is well balanced. If you are assessing the energy with just your hands, you will want to stand up with your client with your main or dominant hand in front of their chakras and your feeling hand in the back of them, so that your hands are on either side of the client. When you channel into the chakra and the energy bounces back immediately onto the hand you are channeling with, that means the chakra is blocked, as the energy cannot get through. If the energy goes in and in and in, then it is depleted. Once the energy goes in for a short while and then bounces back, it is balanced. If you experience static on the hand, the chakra is torn.

173

A torn chakra is one that has been blown out, usually by a trauma or intense confusion or despair. I will often see a torn heart chakra if someone has lost a loved one, either through death or a break up. If someone has had surgery on their stomach, this may result in a torn solar plexus chakra. An abortion can manifest a torn sacral chakra. If someone is severely depressed, they can have a torn 3rd eye or crown chakra. Physical accidents can also result in torn chakras. Taking too many drugs can cause a tear in the 3rd eye or crown. With the amount of high frequency energies that are being sent down to the earth in this year of 2012, I am seeing a lot of torn chakras simply because people are not at a high enough vibration to process these energies and it causes the chakra to blow out, similar to a light bulb being blown out.

If the chakra is torn, you will need to invoke Krysta the healing angel for her golden netting to repair the chakra. Hold your channeling hand out to receive the netting, then when it feels full, channel the golden netting into the chakra until it is repaired. Then channel the appropriate color to complete it, a thought intent and a green bubble.

To begin channeling the energy, hold the dominant hand palm down, over the chakra that is being worked on and in the receiving hand, hold a large quartz crystal facing upward in the palm. The quartz crystal automatically doubles one's electromagnetic field and amplifies the energy that is coming from Source.

At each chakra first channel pure white light energy and set the intention of clearing any negativity from that chakra. Say silently and affirm with your Higher Self, "Allow this white light to cleanse any negativity that is stored here." You may name some of the negativity you wish to clear, such as guilt, anger, frustration, which are all variations on the same theme of fear. Wash the chakra for a few minutes or until you feel that all the dirt or gunk has been cleared away. If a chakra is particularly full of negativity, the energy will feel heavy with a lot of static. As you continue to wash it of debris, the static will become less and less until the energy feels smooth. Always flick the channeling hand toward the rebalancing column at the base of the table to get rid of any excess energy before you start channeling the next color.

Then your Higher Self will tell you what color is needed in this chakra. The basic colors for the chakras are silver for the earth star, red for the base, orange for the sacral, yellow for the solar plexus, green and pink for the heart, blue for the throat, indigo for the third eye, violet for the crown and platinum for the soul star. When you are channeling energy into the body, you should project a thought intent into the color i.e.; releasing inflammation, clearing emotional pain from this center, releasing stress in the neck area, healing sore knee, healing the heart, forgiveness, hope, trust, compassion, bringing clarity and focus to the mind, opening the channel for self-expression, strengthening the will to succeed, etc. Listen to your Higher Self for what thought intent is needed here, they always know! Once you have finished channeling the color into that chakra, you then channel green to create a bubble to surround the thought intent. The green bubble acts as a sealant for the intention.

Listen to what your Higher Self tells you this chakra needs. If you are starting out, you will need to be patient for the information being sent to you, always trust the first bit of information you receive, don't second guess your Higher Self. Once you gain a clear feeling of what is going on in that center, begin talking to the client about what you are feeling or picking up on.

For example; if I am working on the sacral chakra, the word "guilt" will pop into my head and I may ask my Higher Self for clarification of what the guilt is being caused by. I will then be given an image of a man and get the feeling of an angry man so I will say to my client, "What is the issue you have with guilt? I may say something like, "Is there an angry man in your life who made you feel guilty?" Often just saying a couple of sentences like these will be enough to trigger the discussion and the client will respond with "Yes, my dad used to hit me when I was a child and I hated him for that and I feel guilty for hating him because he's my dad and I love him too." Then we will discuss this subject further, all the while I am channeling energy into that center with the thought form of releasing guilt. If we get to the root of the problem in the discussion, then that person will quite often feel a shift, a release occurring in that center. In this case, with this particular issue, I would tune into the situation and say something like, "Your father did what he himself was taught, he himself carried an enormous amount of pain inside of him because his father did the same thing to him and he never

177

forgave him. Knowing how much pain he was in, you can then have compassion for his actions. It is necessary to accept that this happened and release your anger toward your father for his behavior in order for you to move on."

The unforgiveness that the client has for their father may be stored in their heart center, which you will later discover as you work your way up through the chakras. This discussion focuses on the big picture and the truth of the situation rather than just understanding it from the client's single point of view. Often what appears at the time to be a terrible event or situation can later on turn out to be a blessing in disguise.

Forgiveness is a key ingredient to healing, you simply cannot move fully forward in your own life until you have forgiven everyone, yourself included. It is not necessarily something that can be done in one session, it may take time to truly forgive, but it may also happen quickly, so we can't limit the healing by our time projections. Everyone is different, let the person experience whatever they need to and in whatever timeframe in order to heal.

It is important to note here, that your intuition and your connection with your Higher Self is the key factor that is guiding the session. As you continue to connect with your Higher Self through meditation, your ability to receive accurate information about your client will grow.

Work your way up through the chakras one by one first cleansing with white light, followed by the appropriate color to balance as well as any pertinent discussion that is needed to address any issues. The information you will be given from your Higher Self is always different and can be related to all levels. You may receive information about the client's physical condition, for example, if a woman has had a hysterectomy, I may be shown a visual of the reproductive system with a pair of scissors.

I will then ask if the client had surgery in her reproductive area and a discussion will begin on that subject. She may have bad feelings about the surgery, feeling less of a woman now that her uterus has been removed. Or there may be residual effects of the surgery itself, at which point I would clear those energies and talk to her body, asking it to accept the new form it has taken on with the reproductive organ no longer intact. I may ask the client to take her awareness to that area and talk to the body and see what response she gets. Then ask her to send that area love and acceptance, while also affirming this in her mind or out loud. I would then be channeling pink into the area for love and acceptance at which point the client may feel a shift.

The information that comes to you quite often will be on the emotional level, when you are dealing with all sorts of unresolved issues such as guilt, anger, fear, sadness, frustration, abandonment, grief, and the list goes on and on. While discussing these issues, always let your Higher Self guide you because the discussion will come from a higher soul perspective of pure love rather than the mind's limited view.

There is also the spiritual realm of healing that goes way beyond anything we are equipped with understanding here on earth. There are many dimensions and past lives that we are dealing with that only your Higher Self will be able to discuss with the person. For example; a client I was working with had a lot of fear around travel, she was fearful when anyone in her family was traveling to the point of obsession. This fear was causing her and her family great distress. While working on her, a vision was shown to me that in a recent past life she lost her entire family when they died on a boat that sank. When this was revealed to her, she was able to connect with that past life and understand why her fear in this life was so immense. She reported to me a few weeks later that when her sister and niece were traveling, she didn't even think twice about it whereas before, she would have tracked their every move and been uneasy till they walked through the door. The simple awareness of and connection to that truth along with the energetic clearing and rebalancing shifted that fear from her being in this lifetime.

Continue to cleanse and rebalance each chakra and once you reach the top chakra, the crown chakra, cleanse it with white light, like the others, channel the appropriate color.

The next step is to align the person's astral body. An astral body is a spiritual, etheric or energetic body of the physical body. The way we realign the astral bodies is by calling upon the Guardians of Light. They are a team of healers that work specifically with our astral body. Channel purple into the top of the head and ask the Guardians of Light to realign the astral body. You do this by saying, "Guardians of Light, please realign Sarah's astral body.

Cleanse and re-balance any astral body entanglements and make sure that all those entanglements of other people's are cleansed and rebalanced and returned to them. When you have finished with this task, you are free to go with love and thanks."

Next widen and strengthen their path or bridge between the lower self and the Higher Self. Another way of looking at this energetically is to imagine a tunnel or tube that connects from the top of your head to your Higher Self on the third level of the astral plane. This tube exists at birth. If it is not developed the tunnel will become very slight and the connection to the Higher Self is weak, as a result, a person will be too much "in their head" or too logical and unable to access their intuition. This tube or tunnel is the energy pathway that we expand each time we meditate. For people with strong links to their Higher Self who meditate regularly, there will be a very large and wide energetic pathway established. For those who have a weaker tube, channel silver into the pathway to expand and strengthen the bond with the thought intent of connecting this person to the Higher Self.

Next, channel golden light directly into the brain, stimulating all the parts of the brain and in particular, the pituitary and pineal glands. The golden energy will expand these glands which governs our intuition and connection with our Higher Self, and the Divine consciousness. Use the golden light to balance the left brain and right brain equally, the intellect and intuition, as well as activating the corpus collosum, the bridge between both hemispheres of the brain to create a better balance. As the golden light expands, it is working at a DNA level to transmute any negative thoughts and patterns (samskaras) of behavior that no longer serve us and to bring us more fully into our God consciousness. This golden light assists with supporting transformation.

When you have finished channeling color and intent into each chakra and realigning the astral bodies it's important to go back and check the chakras to see if they are balanced. Using the pendulum, see if they are all open and spinning with a balanced frequency. You may need to go back to a particular chakra and work on it further. Once each of the chakras is balanced, you can ask your Higher Self what else is needed to complete the healing.

You may put energetic bubbles around the subject if they need certain energy to help them at this time i.e.; say John is lacking courage to leave his job even though he is miserable and wants to quit but is fearful, then you would channel a yellow bubble around his entire aura with the thought intent of self-confidence to stimulate his will.

In the case of people who are really sick or emotionally distraught, you can also invoke healing angels to stay with them for a certain period of time. Ask an angel who identifies with this person to please come forward and let themselves be known. Ask for them to give you a name because it is always helpful for a client to have a name to identify their angel by - it makes it more personal for them since they usually can't see the angel. When the angel comes forward and identifies itself, ask the angel to help this person with whatever they are going through at the time and allot a specific time limit, say a few days or a week or a month or till the next energy session. Thank the angel and then advise your subject that the angel is there for them and that they can talk to them about anything that they need help with. Angels are always available to us and we can always talk to them and ask them for help with anything. The angel will be there to help that person heal and also provide comfort, support and unconditional love. That is why I will invoke a specific angel at the end of an energy session. Thank you angels!!

Next, channel a golden light and bubble around the subject with the intention of attracting abundance of all good things. Abundance is our birthright and it's a gift to that person to envelop them in gold and send them out to the world with that frequency resonating, it's also a nice way to finish a session. When you have finished, check with the subject to see how they are feeling and if they feel ok. If they feel "off" or "weird" talk to them and see if you can uncover the source of what is not right and then take the necessary steps to ensure they feel comfortable before you finish.

Finally, wash yourself and the subject in white light again and then ask your Higher Self to protect your client with a layer of blue light, purple light and golden light and then seal your energy with three golden rings coming from the top of their head, around their bodies and entire aura and down into their earth. Do the same for yourself. This protects and seals your energy so you aren't picking up other's "stuff". It also protects you from any entities that are attracted to your light. Once both your energies have been sealed with the golden rings, you can remove the green energy mat and flick it up the column out to the Universe, knowing that it will be cleansed and rebalanced and used for healing for whatever you have dedicated it for. Once you send this energy back to the Universe for rebalancing, seal the point of exit with your dominant hand. Now the room is clean of all the excess, negative energy.

Acknowledge and give thanks to the light beings, it is essential and they love it! Also remember to give thanks to your client and yourself.

The body will respond to Vibrational healing very quickly, unless it is extremely depleted of energy. If is depleted then we must work on rebuilding the balance of energy throughout all the chakra centers, which will then enable the body to fight off disease quickly. You always have to double check the effect of your energy work on your client before you let them leave - if they need additional topping up or adjustments, you will need to make sure this happens.

Working with Children and Animals

If you are working with children, only use half the amount of energy you use for an adult and channel only white light for a short period of time. If you are working with animals, you must ask your Higher Self to align the energy you are channeling with the Angelic Kingdom and then channel only white light into the animal. When you have finished, you ask that you be re-aligned and attuned to the spiritual alignment of healing that works with human beings.

This method of how to channel the love light source energy to help others heal themselves is a system I learned in the school in Australia and I added my own style using oils, crystals and counseling from my Higher Self. I encourage you to create your own style of working with your client, make it your own. You will find what works for you and your client by the hours you spend working with them. Have fun with this, it is a gift!

<u>Energetic Exercise</u>: Pink Balloon

This is an exercise to release negative thoughts - it is called the pink balloon exercise. Visualize a pink balloon above your head. Now feel all your negativity, anger and frustration rising up into this balloon and see the balloon filling with that negativity and repeat: "It is my free-will and choice to remove and release all negative thought forms from my aura. I call upon my Higher Self and the Universal Healers and ask that this negative thought form be disconnected from me and that the energy be turned into positive energy and returned to the physical plane for planetary healing." Take a nice deep breath and relax. Visualize the balloon above your head with a thick white cord connecting the balloon to the top of your head. Now take a pair of silver scissors and cut the cord. Take a nice deep breath and as you exhale, see and feel the balloon filled with negative energy floating away from you and off into the distance and finally out of sight. By using this simple technique regularly, we can keep negative thought forms from building up.

Chapter Fourteen - Crystals and Essential Oils

I incorporate crystals and essential oils into my Vibrational healing session because both work with the body and energy field of the person to raise their frequency. They are assisting me and my Higher Self in the work of rebalancing the person's energy field. It is not imperative that you use either in a healing session, but I love both and find them to be extremely valuable.

Crystals

Crystals are amazing healing tools and the best way to work with a crystal, just like people, is to form a relationship with it. Crystals respond to love and their purpose is to help us heal, they love to serve.

Each crystal carries with it a different vibration, depending on the part of the earth it was formed in, that corresponds to a different chakra. Within each crystal there exists a spirit or deva and by connecting with this deva, you will receive guidance for healing.

You must always cleanse your crystals first before you program them to work with a particular issue. Crystals absorb and

189

transmit energy and one of their functions is to cleanse and transmute negative energies. If you do not cleanse your crystals they will become saturated and unable to do their work.

There are a few ways to cleanse a crystal.

1. Place them on a bed of amethyst.
2. Place them in cold salt water over night.
3. You can hold the crystal under cold running water and with your mind, see it being cleansed.
4. Put a few drops of essential oil on the crystal such as lavender, eucalyptus and rosemary and rub them with a soft, clean cloth.
5. Smudge them with a sage stick.
6. Pass them through the light of a candle.

I also like to leave crystals out under a full moon, or in the day time sun, depending on what energy you want to charge the crystal with, feminine or masculine. You can also bury a crystal in the earth or leave it in water, including the ocean.

Once you have cleansed the crystal you will need to program it

for whatever you wish it to do, for example: program an

aquamarine crystal to work with the third eye chakra in helping

that person connect with their intuitive wisdom or higher

guidance.

To Program a Crystal:

1. Open up and clear your mind of all thought, take a deep breath and center yourself.
2. Hold the crystal in your left hand and bring down white light into your crown chakra.
3. Think of the intention you wish to program this crystal with i.e.: to boost confidence in the solar plexus chakra.
4. Communicate this intent and blow the white light three times into the crystal.
5. Close your non-dominant hand around the newly programmed crystal and exclaim with, "And so it is."

Now you can place the crystal on the body where the chakra is. You can use many crystals simultaneously or singularly. Whatever guidance you receive to help heal, balance or shift the chakra. The frequency of the crystal will immediately begin to work with the energy of the chakra, adjusting the vibration to a higher state.

Once you form a relationship with a crystal, you can ask the crystal where on the person's body it needs to go to heal.

Crystals tune into a person's vibration instantly and they will tell you where they want to go; just feel and listen and trust. Always remember to thank the crystals when you are finished with your session! I always place them on a bed of amethyst or citrine for cleansing and rebalancing for the next person. I will also do a monthly cleanse in sea salt water over night.

On the next two pages is a chart of which crystals correspond to chakras. I am only listing a few crystals that I primarily work with. There are many more crystals to choose from. Different people will give you different information on which crystals work best for healing particular issues. I encourage you to explore and try out your crystals on various chakras to discover what works best for you and your clients. Always tell your client you are placing the crystal on them and to let you know if any crystal feels uncomfortable so that you can move it straight away. These are just some of the functions each crystal can perform; there is much, much more information in the various crystal books available on the market.

Chakra	Crystal	Function
Earthstar	Smoky quartz	Clears negativity, grounding, helps one to be in the present moment
	Obsidian	Detoxifies, helps with arthritis, brings up major life issues to work on
	Hematite	Promotes balance, aides blood problems
Root	Mother Earth stone	Stimulates life force & will to live, nurtures
	Mugglestone	For energy, balance, security & strength
	Obsidian	For grounding & protection
	Tiger's Eye	Encourages optimism and discipline
Sacral	Chrysoprase	Stimulates fertility & balances male, female energies, heals a broken heart
	Rose quartz	Emotional healing of any abuse
	Fluorite	Encourages self love & unconditional love Draws off negative emotions
	Carnelian	Restores vitality and motivation, enhances sexuality

Solar Plexus	Rutilated quartz	Helps to strengthen will
	Labradorite	Heals digestive disorders
	Citrine	Helps manifest abundance, heal addiction issues and boosts self confidence
Heart	Rose quartz	Promotes unconditional and self love
	Chrysoprase	Heals broken hearts
	Aventurine	Instills tenderness and fosters love
	Rhodonite	Helps you feel loving and stay in your heart
Throat	Sodalite	Cleanses lymph system, promotes harmony between conscious and unconscious minds
	Lapis Lazuli	Encourages power of the spoken word
	Turquoise	Helps articulate emotional issues, linking intuitive inspiration with self-expression
3rd Eye	Fluorite	Promotes concentration, draws off chaos
	Aquamarine	Helps connect one to Higher Self
	Labradorite	Reduces stress & anxiety,

	Moonstone	Balances emotions, enhances intuition
	Lapis Lazuli	Promotes serenity & spiritual attainment, clears headaches
Crown	Selenite	Promotes oneness with the Universe
	Clear quartz crystal	Amplifies and transmits higher frequencies
	Amethyst	Protective & highly spiritual. Calming
Trans-personal Point	Selenite	Draws forth angelic energy, removes blocks

<u>Essential Oils</u>

I use essential oils during the Vibrational healing sessions to help raise the frequency of the chakras. Essential oils have their own frequency. All atoms in the universe have vibrational motion. Each periodic motion has a "frequency", (the number of oscillations per second), measured in Hertz:

1 Hertz (Hz) = 1 oscillation per second (ops)

1 Kilo Hertz (KHz) = 1,000 ops

1 Mega Hertz (MHz) = 1,000,000 ops or 1 million

1 Giga Hertz (GHz) = 1,000,000,000 ops or 1 billion

1 Tetra Hertz (THz) = 1,000,000,000,000 ops or 1 trillion

Essential oils are measured in Megahertz frequencies. Essential oil frequencies start at 52 MHz and go as high as 320 MHz. Rose (Rosa damascena) essential oil has the highest of all the oils at 320 MHz. Please keep in mind that frequencies of essential oils vary according to each batch, growing conditions, soil and weather conditions.

Essential oils align frequencies, thus balancing and harmonizing body organs. Mixing or blending essential oils amplifies these frequencies; this is called "synergy", which is a natural way to increase the body's electrical frequency.

Clinical research shows that essential oils have the highest frequency of any natural substance known to man, creating an environment in which disease; bacteria, virus, fungus, etc. cannot live. Essential oil frequencies are several times greater than frequencies of herbs, foods and even the human body.

Another worthy point is the influence that thoughts have on our frequency as well. Negative thoughts lowered the measured frequency by 12 MHz and positive thoughts raised the measured frequency by 10 MHz. It was also found that prayer and meditation increased the measured frequency levels by 15 MHz.

Essential Oils are multifunctional so they have a wide spectrum of application. They work for the need that is present. If there is no need present in the body, there is minimal reaction. While oils are not accumulative in the body, their frequency and effect is cumulative. They are made of the same substances the body is made of - they are non-toxic.

Essential oils are absorbed and go to work within seconds in the body. Layering the oils in application, and the addition of heat produces faster penetration and results. Essential oils stay in a healthy body up to eight hours."

Below is a chart that can help you with choosing essential oils to help rebalance the chakras. Please know your oils, learn which ones cannot be applied directly to the skin and need a carrier oil so as not to cause any irritation to the skin. I focus on three chakras that need rebalancing, using only three oils, any more than that can overwhelm some people who are sensitive to the oils. Apply the oil, 1-3 drops, onto the area of the chakra either on the back or in the front of the body. In the case of the root chakra, apply to the lower part of the spine or onto the feet.

Essential Oil	Chakra
Cardamom, Cedar wood, Clary Sage, Clove, Frankincense, Ginger, Grounding, Patchouli, Purification, Rosewood, Sandalwood, Vetiver	Root or Base
Abundance, Clary Sage, Geranium, Jasmine, Joy, Melissa, Neroli, Patchouli, Rose, Rose Geranium, Tangerine, Ylang Ylang, Vetiver	Sacral
Fennel, Frankincense, Juniper, Helichrysum, Ginger, Lavender, Lemon, Lemongrass, Myrrh, Rosemary, Peppermint, Sandalwood Valor, Vetiver	Solar Plexus
Bergamot, Chamomile, Geranium, Jasmine, Joy, Lavender, Peace & Calming, Rose, Sandalwood, Ylang Ylang	Heart
Frankincense, Geranium, Lavender, Roman Chamomile, Sandalwood, Valor	Throat
Clary Sage, Frankincense, Lavender, Rose	Third Eye
Basil, Frankincense, Jasmine, Lavender, Myrrh, Rose, Ravensara, Rosemary, Sandalwood, Spruce, White Angelica	Crown

Always ask if the person would like the oils, and ask them if there are any oils they do not like before choosing the oils. Let them know that the oil will not stain their clothes. Most people love the oils, but not everyone does, especially super sensitive people. I recommend you buy a reference guide to learn about each individual oil so you know what it is capable of and how to use it correctly. I love essential oils and they will always be a part of my life and my work.

<u>Energetic Exercise:</u> Brain Illumination

Visualize golden light entering into your brain from the crown chakra. See and feel this golden light permeating every single part of the brain. As this golden light flows throughout the brain, it opens up parts of it that have remained closed. Feel it totally enveloping the Spinal Cord, the Medulla Oblongata, Pons, Cerebellum, into the Limbic System, the Amygdala, Hippocampus, Hypothalamus, Thalamus and into the Neocortex, Frontal Lobe, Parietal Lobe, Temporal Lobe, Occipital Lobe, the Corpus Callosum and Broca's Area, the pituitary and pineal glands. Now feel every cell in your brain vibrating with the frequency of this golden light. Feel the golden light entering into the DNA and RNA and clearing any negative programming based on false beliefs and illusions and aligning your entire being with the Truth. Feel every cell energized, invigorated, perfectly healthy and working in harmony with one another. Feel that you are in perfect health.

Chapter Fifteen - The Transformational Process

"This we know; all things are connected like the blood that unites us. We do not weave the web of life, we are merely a strand in it. Whatever we do to the web, we do to ourselves."

˜Chief Seattle

In order for transformation to take place, a person has to want to change. There are many people out there who don't want to change, they are perfectly happy (or not) with the way they are and they don't want to evolve, or grow. We can't force others to change no matter how much we want them to; it has to come from them. Change is scary for a lot of people. If someone does not want to change, it's important to accept it instead of trying to change them or you will suffer.

The one thing that is constant in life is that everything changes, so one may as well accept this reality and embrace it completely. Learn to love change and go with the flow.

There's a saying, "Change will happen when the pain of remaining the same is greater than the pain of the change." It can be so frustrating to watch someone do the same thing over and over and get the same results when you can clearly see a better way forward for them. The frustration has to be significant enough within them to inspire them to act a different way, and commit to that new behavior. I understand this because I stayed stuck for a long time before I was propelled to take action and commit to a new way of life. A person will learn in their own time at their own pace, they need to own the change. Commitment is crucial, because once someone commits themselves; the energy of that decision propels them forward and aligns them with the supportive Universal energy to bring their goal to fruition. If you hesitate or become wishy washy, nothing can manifest because the energy is weak and unstable. Make the decision, commit to it 100% and work continuously toward the goal with the knowingness that it will manifest.

Goethe said, "Until one is committed, there is hesitancy, the chance to draw back, always ineffectiveness. Concerning acts of initiative (and creation) there is one elementary truth the ignorance of which kills countless ideas and splendid plans: That the moment one definitely commits oneself then providence moves too: All sorts of things occur to help one that would

204

otherwise never have occurred. A whole stream of events issues from the decision raising in one's favor all manner of unforeseen incidents and meetings and material assistance which no man could have dreamt would come his way. Whatever you can do, or dream you can, begin it. Boldness has genius, power and magic in it."

Many people seek out Vibrational healing because they are feeling trapped and are not happy with themselves or certain situations in their lives. Part of my goal with clients is to help guide them through the transformation process. I listen to find out where the person is on their journey, what obstacles and challenges they are currently experiencing in their lives and discuss where they want to be and what can they do to bring about this change.

Transformation is about replacing negativity, stagnation and illness with positive thinking, the flow of abundance, joy and good health. First you need to have a clear idea what you want to change, then you need to do everything in your power to manifest these goals in your life. Some of the tools for transformation include eating healthful foods, eliminating toxins,

205

breaking addictions, exercising, yoga, counseling, taking supplements & vitamins, meditating, praying, communing with nature, cultivating healthy relationships in your life including with yourself, Higher Self and the Divine, daily affirmations, visualizations, setting positive intentions, self-love, and identifying with yourself as the Divine within. Thinking about these things is great but to truly transform you must take action. For many, these efforts bring great rewards because profound shifts occur and a new way of life is established. Let's face it; it is hard work, but so incredibly worth it.

Another factor of transformation is keeping our own personal energy system clear and aligned. When we hold a positive vibration of strong intent and we support it with our thoughts and behavior, lasting change can happen. When we do not vibrate at a high frequency and allow fear or negativity to block our receptivity, then we will experience a delay in receiving that which we have asked for until we can clear the blocks and hold the high frequency energy.

The human energy system includes the upward and downward flow of universal energy into the human body and the seven major chakras, or energy vortices, which attach to the spinal column. These parts of our energy system are very dynamic and change quickly based on what we think and feel. If our thoughts are not positive, our energy system reacts by pulling in negative energy and can become blocked. Old behavior patterns repeat themselves, preventing us from moving towards our greatest intentions. When our energy system is clear, however, we are able to project positive energy, one of the key elements required to manifest our dreams.

Remember, no matter how hard the transformation process may feel at times, stay positive, keep the faith and continue to believe in yourself and your dreams and you will succeed! I don't believe you ever get to a place in life where everything is wonderful and you can sit back and say, "I've made it, I have finally arrived." Life just isn't like that. It is in a constant state of flux and there will always be challenges, obstacles and things to work out. You may feel like you're going backwards sometimes, but if you vibrate at a higher state those challenges will no longer be viewed as being a "problem" they will simply be viewed as challenges which are lessons to be learned to help your soul evolve. Life then becomes very interesting and fun.

Only you can make the changes and connect to your soul and to Spirit to uncover the truth of your life and align yourself to live your life according to that truth, with integrity. Only you can choose to raise your vibration and live with love in your heart. Remember no matter what your circumstances, that you are loved and you have help from all the light beings who want you to reach your highest potential. It is your choice. Choose truth, choose light and choose love. Each of these words has the same meaning, truth is light, and light is love. The Truth will set you free.

Understanding Your Life from Your Soul's Perspective

I try and counsel people to view their trials and tribulations from their soul's perspective instead of being caught up in the drama of the human ego mind.

When we look at the bigger picture from soul consciousness rather than ego consciousness, it becomes apparent that everything really does happen for a reason and that most of it is agreed upon between souls within a soul group before birth. These truths of our souls allow us to understand the reasons for the events in our lives, the challenging relationships and apparent 'misfortunes', 'illnesses', 'addictions' or 'accidents' that we encounter in our lifetime. Agreements are planned from a place of pure love with the intention of allowing the soul and everyone in the soul group to evolve.

I have always felt we are in 'earth school', here to learn our lessons. When clients come in they share what they are experiencing from the personality, such as multiple accidents and the chronic pain they carry, the loss of a child or loved one and the crippling grief that accompanies it, financial ruin or unexpected change of fortune that seems to make no sense. When we look at these from a higher perspective, it may provide relief to the personality to know that this was planned by your soul and the souls of all involved. It may also help to remember that what we are experiencing right now will change and it won't always be this way. Take for example Nelson Mandela; he spent 27 years in prison, which would appear to be a terrible misfortune. When he was finally released from incarceration, he became President and chose not to condemn or exclude the very people who imprisoned him, but forgive them and embrace them as equals. His actions on the earthly realm brought peace and love to the hearts and minds of many.

"As we expand our self-concept from personality to soul, we grant ourselves a more accurate understanding. We also shift our focus from the pain caused by life challenges to the wisdom and growth they offer. When we saw pointlessness, now we see purpose. When we saw punishment, now we see a gift. When we saw burden, now we see opportunity. Never again the victims of life, we become the recipients of its many blessings." I love this passage from Robert Schwartz because this concept gives us back our power. These horrible challenges didn't happen to us, punishment from an unloving God; we planned them for our own soul growth. Once you have this awareness, you no longer have to play the role of the victim, you can be fully empowered and truly learn from what is happening.

The idea that our soul lives on eternally really solidified within my consciousness. Of course I had always believed that my soul would live on but I was able to understand that both my parents are still with me, not in the physical but certainly in another dimension, their love and energy is still accessible to me in this lifetime and it dawned on me that WE DON'T DIE. Sure, the body personality of Beth will pass away but our spirit lives on forever. If I don't get my lessons in this life, they will be presented to me again in another life. Mind you, I am all for getting my lessons in this life and evolving as much as possible. When my parents died I felt terrible grief and felt my life could never be as good as it was when they were in it. From the soul's perspective the pain inherent in this learning process is temporary and brief, but the resultant wisdom is literally eternal. But it has now been years since my mom and dad left the earth plane and I am finding my life continues to become more and more beautiful and for that I am eternally grateful.

In terms of our relationships, sometimes you may have a connection with someone that feels very challenging. I ended a relationship with someone as I felt that person did not show respect for me in a way that I deserved. Shortly after the end of the relationship I felt a tremendous amount of self love which I had never known before. I then realized that this apparent "bad relationship" had served to grow unconditional love for myself and that I had planned it with that individual in order for the self love to come about at this point in my life. I could now stop being angry and blaming him and instead thank him at a soul level for serving me. This person is no longer in my life, however, our soul mission was complete and I chose to no longer associate with him.

"When we plan our lives, we choose to 'work' with other souls whom we love very much and who love us. In this way our greatest tormentors are often those with whom we share the most love when in spirit. Gratitude toward those who have most challenged us and thus most stimulated our evolution, is a soul-level perspective we can adopt while still in body. When we make that choice, we remove blame from our lives. Without blame forgiveness becomes possible, and with forgiveness

212

comes healing." This excerpt from Robert Schwartz explains why I kept wanting to be return to the person who wasn't treating me well, it's because my soul knows of great love for his soul, but it wasn't supposed to work out in the this lifetime so I could learn the very important lesson of self love.

Robert Schwartz also talks about living a life of opposites, which is when you live the opposite of what you will become such as a person who experiences the despair and disconnection of life as an addict who then becomes a healer after having learned the great gift of compassion and self love. This is, in fact, my own story. I was so frustrated, confused and miserable back in the days of my addictions when I hated my job, did not know my life purpose, had many failed relationships, treated myself with disrespect and I felt tremendous guilt, shame and self hatred. Deep down I knew something was terribly wrong, but I continued to live a self-destructive lifestyle. Now I live the opposite of that and I am grateful for that time spent even though it was incredibly painful at the time. I'm so glad I didn't give up on myself because otherwise I wouldn't know what it was like to reach the great heights in self respect, self love, compassion for others and the true grace of knowing God that are now part of my life.

I encourage you to choose to view your life through your soul consciousness as this will lift your vibration as well as the vibration of the entire population. For all of mankind's sake, if you are not already awake, wake up! Instead of allowing these apparent difficulties, obstacles and challenges to break you, use them to make you whole. Remember yourself as pure love, "As we enter the physical plane, we are love temporarily hidden from itself. When we remember who we really are, our inner light, our love, shines forth for all to see."

Chapter Sixteen - Working With Your Client

"Doing good to others is not a duty, it is a joy, for it increases our own health and happiness."

~Zoroaster

The one thing that you can count on about giving a Vibrational healing session is that you will never ever know how the person is going to be affected. Everyone feels and reacts to the energy differently and every session is unique. Some people will be blown away by the experience just as I was and some people will not consciously feel anything at all except maybe more relaxed. However, no matter what their outward reaction is, there is great healing taking place in their energy field that they may never know on a conscious level.

Other healers, light workers and very sensitive people tend to feel the energy more, just as they do in everyday life. The important thing to remember here is that even if the client does not feel anything, the energy is still benefiting them. Sometimes people will report feeling a shift a week or two later or they will just say that they feel more grounded and calmer, making it easier for them to deal with whatever is going on in their lives. Others will tell me that they experienced huge life changes and were able to make dramatic shifts. The most consistent effect the energy has on everyone is that it instills a deep sense of inner peace.

I've had sessions where the energy of deceased relatives comes through me and I get an impression of who is there and will share that with the client. When this occurs, it feels as if I've just stuck my finger in an electric socket and I feel very amped up. I then tune into the energy and relay any information that is being downloaded to me. For me it comes in images, thoughts and feelings, for others practicing this it may come in whatever modality you are most aligned with be it clairvoyance (seeing), clairaudience (hearing), claircognizance (knowing), or clairsentience (feeling).

The first thing I do with a client is talk to them and find out what they hope to achieve with the session. Are they having physical problems or emotional difficulties, are they struggling with addiction, are they suffering from grief? I try to gain a clear understanding of their current problem or challenge through discussion. Often other stuff will come up later during the session as your Higher Self feeds you images, feelings or tells you what they are holding onto in their energy centers. Once you have identified what it is they would like to change or accomplish with the session i.e.; stress relief, more mental clarity and focus, grounding, increased creativity; then you can work to bring about this desired change. It will also give you an idea of what thought intentions to channel into the chakras. You can schedule further appointments depending on how the client reacts to the energy.

I always like to make the next appointment before the client leaves and then will discuss with them what shifts and changes took place following the previous session. As far as spacing out the sessions, it depends on the client. Some people like to rebalance every 2 or 3 weeks, or for others it's once a month. If you're working with a very ill person, you will want to schedule sessions more often, maybe once a week till they are feeling better. I try not to push, but suggest a time for the next session according to what your Higher Self says and then let the client decide what is best for them.